The Impact of Israel's Founding Myths on The Prospects for a Two-State Solution

by

Andrew J Winnick
Professor of Economics & Statistics,
California State University, Los Angeles
and
President, The American Institute for Progressive Democracy

© 2015

ISBN : 1523923709
ISBN: 978-1523923700

Abstract

This study asks readers interested in the Israeli-Palestinian conflict to accept the challenge to consider the well-documented facts presented, and, in that light, to (re)evaluate their understanding of:

1) The circumstances that led to the founding of the State of Israel
2) The nature of the war fought between Israel's founders and both the Palestinians and the Arab forces that invaded from five surrounding nations
3) The history of the negotiations over the last 25 years to try to arrive at a Two-State Solution

The analysis is pursued by examining fifteen myths. Evidence is presented that these are indeed are myths, that the statements are not true, no matter how firmly many people believe in them or how often they are repeated. It is argued that the (false) belief in these myths leads to many of the problems in negotiating a Two-State Solution. The hope is expressed that the corollary is also true: that the sooner it is understood that these are indeed myths, the sooner it may be possible for the two sides to find their way to successful negotiations toward two states.

Following a short introduction that seeks to place this study into a broader context, there is a list of the fifteen myths with page references. In the context of examining these myths, a series of embedded topics are identified and analyzed, including:

- the nature of the British Mandate over Palestine
- the actual role of the U.N. in the formation of Israel
- the history of Jewish and Palestinian nationalism
- the relative strengths and actions of the settler/Israeli forces and those of the Palestinians and five invading Arab nations in 1947-49, especially concerning the charges of ethnic cleansing and massacres
- a brief overview of the results of the past negotiations toward a Two-State Solution
- the nature and makeup of the current (2015-16) Israeli government
- the effect of that government's demand for recognition of Israel as a "Jewish State"
- an examination of Theodor Herzl's use of the term "Jewish State"
- the nature of and problems within the Palestinian leadership
- the impact of the 2015 dispute over the Iran nuclear agreement
- the role of the charge of anti-Semitism in deflecting criticism of the Israeli government's policies in the context of the U.S. State Department's definition of anti-Semitism

At the end there are seven appendices with charts and maps. At the very end is a brief bio concerning the author's background.

The expressed goal of this work is to pull together what are often disparate analyses of these many topics in the hope of stimulating learning and discussions that will better enable concerned persons to propel movement toward the establishment of two states, Israel and Palestine, both enjoying peace, security and economic development. In that spirit, the reader is encouraged to consider disseminating this work to friends and colleagues.

Access to this work on the web, in print, or as an ebook

Reproduction Rights

The Impact of Israel's Founding Myths on
The Prospects for a Two-State Solution

by

Andrew J Winnick
Professor of Economics and Statistics, California State University – Los Angeles
President, The American Institute for Progressive Democracy (taipd.org)
(andy.winnick@gmail.com)

Introduction

"…what you should really look for…is intellectual integrity: the willingness to admit mistakes and change course… the willingness to entertain different ideas…I'm not calling for an end to ideology…What you should seek, in yourself and others, is not an absence of ideology but an open mind, willing to consider the possibility that parts of the ideology may be wrong." Paul Krugman in *Ideology and Integrity*, NY Times, May 1, 2015

There have been many books and papers (including my own) that discuss the prospects for the implementation of a Two-State Solution to the Israeli-Palestinian conflict and why it has not happened. This failure is despite the fact that (as I will describe later) both sides have discussed, and have known full well for years, almost all the terms of such a solution. Why is it the case that many Palestinians and Israelis, and their governments, have at various times shown very little willingness to move toward a Two-State Solution to solve their conflict? Why is it, on the other hand, that there have been times when one side or the other, sometimes both, have demonstrated more willingness, but then one side or the other walked away? One can clearly focus on the Palestinians and such valid and important issues as the weak Palestinian leadership, the split between Fatah and Hamas, the split within Hamas between the political and military leadership, and the lack of trust on the part of Palestinians concerning Israelis' willingness (maybe even in their ability) to implement any agreement they signed. All of these problems on the Palestinian side have been talked and written about in great detail. And indeed, in the third part of this work, we will return to this topic. But in the first two parts of this work, I want to focus on another, too often overlooked, aspect of this problem on the Israeli side.

In thinking more about why Israel seems to lack a strong political will to reach a settlement that would lead to a Two-State Solution it seems to me that, at least in part, it is fear. There is a deeply felt, almost existential fear that permeates much of Israeli Jewish society and also impacts the American Jewish community. This is a view of Israel as a small and relatively weak David that faces the larger, stronger Goliath of the Palestinians, who are backed by the 21 other nations that compose the Arab League, plus non-Arab Iran. Given the current relative effective strength of the Israeli military as compared to the combined militaries of the Arab states, and given the history of the last 70 years in which Israel has clearly and decisively won every military conflict, the question is why there is such an ingrained sense of victimhood and weakness embedded not only in the Jewish citizens of Israel and in that state, but also in the Jewish diaspora, including many, if not most, American Jews. I would argue that this fear, this sense of victimhood, is at the root of the unwillingness of many Israelis and their government to reach a settlement that would create two states, Israel and Palestine, even though there exists bountiful evidence that such a settlement would accrue to the benefit of Israel - economically, internationally, morally, politically and even militarily.

1

There have been many books written about the repeated persecutions of the Jewish people and their subsequent sense of victimhood. Leaving aside the biblical period, this history goes back to the Babylonian expulsion (597 BCE), the Muslim invasions into what is now Israel/Palestine in the 600s CE, the pogroms in the Pale of Settlement in Eastern Europe, and in Russia and Ukraine (much of the 1800s and early 1900s), the deep anti-Semitism that led to Jewish expulsions from France (1182), England (1290), Spain (1492) and Portugal (1496), to cite only the best known. There were also expulsions of Jews from settlements in the American colonies in the 1700s. And to this we must add the discriminatory laws and housing covenants that pervaded American, British and French history from the early 1800s through the post-World War II period, and such infamous events as the Dreyfus Affair in France (1894-1906). Then, of course, there are the systemic horrors of the Holocaust. These are all well-known and often discussed. In fact, these all have been so well explored that I feel no need to repeat those discussions here. Instead, I want to focus on another factor that feeds the sense of Jewish victimhood: the myths and false historical memories associated with the history of Zionism and with the creation of the State of Israel

I recognize that this is a sensitive subject, even today, because so many American, Israeli and other Jews still firmly believe these founding myths to be true. I argue that all too many Jews base their feelings about Israel and its victimhood, its presumed weakness and vulnerability even today, on the false foundation that is built upon these myths. These myths also lie at the root of Jewish attitudes toward Palestinians and their demands. These feelings unfortunately color peoples' seemingly rational analysis of the current situation and support their lack of a commitment, even their lack of willingness, to move toward a Two-State Solution. An analysis of these founding myths and their impact today is the focus of the first two sections of this paper.

In the third section, I briefly discuss some myths about the Two-State negotiation process as it has played out these last 15-20 years, ending with an analysis of the likely course of future negotiations. I include a discussion of the new Israeli government that was elected in March 2015 and the position of the various parties regarding a Two-State Solution. In this context, I also look briefly at the role these myths play in the nature of Israel's unsuccessful and self-destructive opposition to the recently (summer 2015) negotiated international agreement regarding Iran and nuclear weapons. Finally I discuss the difficult topic of anti-Semitism and how the charge of anti-Semitism has been used, often cynically in my view, to cloak the actions of the Israeli government.

Immediately following this introduction, I provide a list of the fifteen myths that will be examined, and some of the sub-topics that will also be discussed – all with page references for those who want to turn to a particular topic. There are also seven appendixes at the end with charts and maps that are referenced in the examination of the myths.

The purpose of this booklet is to provide information in a format that is useful to provoke thoughtful discussions among people who are not necessarily experts. It is not meant as an academic paper, so there are no footnotes or endnotes. However, embedded throughout the discussion will be found references to the particular sources used, and sometimes to other suggested readings. I have tried to do this in a manner that does not distract from the flow of the presentation of each topic, while at the same time keeping the references close to where the relevant discussion occurs. There are also numerous subheadings throughout to help the reader keep track of where they are in the analysis, and to help in going back to find where a particular topic is discussed.

Keeping in mind the Krugman quote at the beginning of this paper concerning intellectual integrity and the need to keep an open mind, I recognize that it is difficult for all of us to reconsider narratives that we have long accepted as valid. But in the face of contrary, provable facts, intellectual integrity demands that we make that effort. Of course, sometimes one can challenge the validity of one set of facts with opposing facts, but intellectual integrity demands that we do not simply refuse to consider evidence contrary to our convictions. It is my hope that this work will encourage the reconsideration of these myths and provoke useful discussions.

Andy Winnick
Claremont, CA
September, 2015

The List of Myths and Other Topics Examined
Part I - The Period Prior to the Declaration of Israeli Independence

Part II - The War* of Independence / Al Nakba (The Catastrophe)
and the Founding of the State of Israel
*Actually two wars: the Civil War (November 1947 - May 1948)
and the War of Independence (May 1948 – February 1949)

The List of Myths and Other Topics Examined (continued)

Part I – The Myths about the Period Prior to the Founding of Israel

The First Foundational Myth: Palestine – "A Land without People for a People without Land"

This was an often heard slogan of the early Zionist movement, coined in 1914 by Israel Zangwill, an ardent Zionist -- that is, by someone who was fervently committed to the creation of a Jewish national homeland in Palestine. But this statement is flagrantly false, and more importantly, it was known by much of the Zionist leadership of the time not to be true. Consider the following evidence, taking particular note of the dates. I have added some emphasis to key passages.

After a visit to Palestine in **1891**, the Jewish essayist Ahad Ha'am wrote:
> **"From abroad, we are accustomed to believe that Eretz Israel is presently almost totally desolate, an uncultivated desert**, and that anyone wishing to buy land there can come and buy all he wants**. But in truth it is not so. In the entire land, it is hard to find tillable land that is not already tilled**; only sandy fields or stony hills, suitable at best for planting trees or vines and, even that after considerable work and expense in clearing and preparing them- only these remain unworked. ... Many of our people who came to buy land have been in Eretz Israel for months, and have toured its length and width, without finding what they seek."

Lawrence Oliphant, who visited Palestine in **1887**, wrote that Palestine's Valley of Esdraelon was
> **"a huge green lake of waving wheat, with its village-crowned mounds rising from it like islands;** and it presents one of the **most striking pictures of luxuriant fertility which it is possible to conceive."**

According to Paul Masson, a French economic historian,
> **"Wheat shipments from the Palestinian port of Acre had helped to save southern France from famine on numerous occasions in** the seventeenth and eighteenth centuries.**"**

Then there is the well documented **history of the Jaffa orange**. This sweet and unique fruit was apparently first developed by Palestinian farmers in the Jaffa area in the mid-1800s, and by the 1850s there are British consular reports of shipments to Europe. Reports indicate that exports grew from around 200,000 in 1845 to **over 38 million in 1870**, and the Jaffa Orange label emerged in 1871, all long before the first wave of Zionist settlers. It is a myth that it was the Jewish settlers that developed and began exporting Jaffa oranges, though they did bring some improved farming techniques and expanded production. It becomes clear as to why this history is not well known when one considers, for example, a recent (June 21, 2015) article in the Israeli newspaper Haaretz about the discovery of an old wall sign in Jaffa that had been buried for years under many layers of paint: "The writing on the wall also evokes the story of Arab citriculture, which has been deleted from Israeli textbooks." The article went on to quote the Israeli artist who was called in to restore the fresco as saying: "We were raised on the stories of Israeli citrus exports under the famous 'Jaffa' brand, but we know very little about the Arab citrus growers." The article also quotes Dr. Nahum Karlinsky, from Ben-Gurion University's Research Institute for the Study of Israel and Zionism as saying: "The citrus industry is perceived in the Israeli consciousness as an exclusively Zionist pioneering effort. In fact, the Palestinian-Arab citrus industry predated it, and in most of the period until 1948, exceeded it in both physical area and quantity of exports."

In fact, during the 1800s and throughout the period of the British Mandate, Jaffa was the largest city in Palestine and was always a majority Palestinian city and the center of Palestinian cultural life. For these reason, the 1947 United Nations General Assembly recommendation to partition Palestine (which is discussed in detail later) called for Jaffa to be in Palestine. But Jewish settler military forces conquered Jaffa and its environs in the months **prior** to the Israeli declaration of independence in May, 1948, forced the 4,000 to 5,000 remaining Palestinians (out of a pre-war population of more than 70,000 in the city, and thousands more in the surrounding areas) into a single neighborhood (al-Ajami) that was surrounded by barbed wire and became known by the Israelis as "the ghetto." However, at this point in this narrative, the key issue is that the early Zionist leaders knew about the extensive Palestinian citrus industry in and around Jaffa even as they talked about Palestine as a land without people.

The fact that the early Zionist leaders knew full well about the native Arab/Palestinian population is demonstrated by their own statements as well. For example, David Ben-Gurion, an early Zionist leader and the first Prime Minister of Israel said in **1937**, as quoted in *Ben Gurion and the Palestine Arabs*, Oxford University Press, 1985: **"We must expel Arabs and take their place."**

Then as reported by Nahum Goldmann (a Zionist leader) in *Le Paradox Juif* (The Jewish Paradox): David Ben-Gurion, once acknowledged that:

"Were I an Arab leader, I would wage perpetual war with Israel."

Ben-Gurion went on to say:

"Sure, God promised it [Palestine] to us, but what does that matter to them? There has been anti-Semitism, Hitler, the Nazis, Auschwitz, but was that their fault? **They only see one thing: We have come here and stolen their country.**" (Emphasis added.)

Moshe Dayan (Chief of Staff of the Israel Defense Force and later Defense Minister, who led military forces in 1948 and 1967) in an address at the Technion University, Haifa, as reported in Haaetz (April 4, 1969):

"**Jewish villages were built in the place of Arab villages.** You do not even know the names of these Arab villages, and I do not blame you because [those] geography books no longer exist. Not only do the books not exist, the Arab villages are not there either. Nahlal arose in the place of Mahlul; Kibbutz Gvat in the place of Jibta; Kibbutz Sarid in the place of Huneifis; and Jefar Yegyshuain in the place of Tal al-Shuman. **There is not a single place built in this country that did not have a former Arab population.**" (Emphasis added)

Examine the population numbers in the table in **Appendix A**. The Zionist leaders knew as they advocated for Jews to move from Europe to Palestine in order to permanently settle there that this was **not** a call to settle in unoccupied, uninhabited land, but was instead an act of colonialism - an effort to displace an indigenous people and take over and rule as much of their land as possible. Keeping in mind that the late 1800s and early 1900s were the peak of the colonial period when Europeans were taking over and dividing among themselves all of Africa and South America, perhaps the plan of the Zionists did not seem particularly problematic. In colonialism everywhere, the local populations were not to be respected, but to be manipulated and used, and if necessary killed. If one thinks about what the Americans who came from Europe did to "the Indians" during the 1800s, what the Zionists did in Palestine was no worse, and, in fact, they behaved much more humanely toward the Palestinians. But nevertheless, it was intentional colonialization, and not to acknowledge that is to base the creation of Israel on a false foundation that denies the validity of the prior claims to that land by the Palestinians. Moreover, this denial of history provides a false sense of the morality of the claims by the European Zionists to the land of Palestine. This refusal to acknowledge, even today, the moral, political and economic primacy of the Palestinians' claim to "their" land is at the heart of much of the tensions in Israel itself today with regard to the Palestinian Israeli citizens, and to the attitude of Israeli and American Jews toward the Occupied Palestinian Territories (the official U.N. designation for the West Bank and Gaza areas).

At the same time, it needs to be acknowledged that in most waves of immigration, there are both push and pull factors, and that was certainly true for the Zionists. That movement was not motivated only by the pull of establishing a national homeland, but also by the push of the conditions many of them faced in Europe, with the widespread pogroms in Eastern Europe and the virulent anti-Semitism almost everywhere in Europe in the late 1800s and during the first half of the 1900s. But read again the quotes from Ben-Gurion above – the Palestinians did not cause the pogroms any more than they were responsible for the Holocaust. Regardless of the motivation for leaving their homeland, those who become colonists in someone else's land, simply do not have any justification for the mistreatment of the native inhabitants of that land. Some of the Zionists as early as the 1930s understood this and pushed for a respectful relationship with the Palestinians and for the creation of two states. Uri Avnery, a peace activist still today, who fought in the 1947-48 wars, served in the Knesset and edited a progressive magazine, is a prime example. But their voices were sadly in a small minority.

Myth #2: The Population of Palestine was Primarily Jewish Prior to the Rise of Zionism in the late 1800s

This too is false. There indeed were Jews living in Palestine continuously from at least 597 BCE, the time of the expulsion from Babylon. (One could make a strong case for Jews having been there thousands of years earlier, but let us not get into the biblical period.) Moreover, there were Jews living in what is now Iraq, Syria, Egypt and Yemen, and some as far west across North Africa as Morocco, from no later than 600-700 CE until today, though after 1947 many immigrated to Israel and elsewhere. These are known as Mizrahi (Eastern or Oriental) Jews (and they still live in Israel). They spoke Arabic in their daily lives, though they knew and used Hebrew in the synagogues. They dressed as Arabs, and they considered themselves to be Arab Jews.

In addition, Jews had lived in southwestern Spain (Andalusia) for many centuries before 700 CE. However, following the expulsion by the Catholics of the Jews and the Moors from Spain in 1492, these Jews, known as Sephardic Jews, migrated to Morocco, then across North Africa to the Middle East (including Palestine), Turkey, Greece and Bulgaria. In North Africa and the Middle East, these Sephardic Jews joined the Mizrahi Jewish communities easily, since many already knew Arabic. The Moors came to Spain in 711, largely from Morocco, North Africa and Mali, and most spoke a dialect of Arabic. Some spoke one of the Berber languages as well. Jews were already in Spain long before the Moors came, and spoke Spanish and/or Ladino (a blend of Spanish and Hebrew). Living in peace beside the Moors from 711 to 1492, most also knew Arabic, making the later integration of the Mizrahi and the Sephardic Jews a relatively smooth process. As they lived in countries in North Africa and the Middle East, virtually all came to speak Arabic and, as with the Mizrahi Jews, came to consider themselves Arab Jews. The two groups together are sometimes also referred to as Oriental Jews.

So as the European Jews, known as Ashkenazi Jews, came to Palestine in the late 1800s and through the post-World War I and II periods, it was these Arab Jews whom they engaged there. The European/Ashkenazi Jews often behaved as if they felt themselves to be far more "civilized" than the Arab Jews who looked and often sounded like Arabs and lived comfortably among the Arabs. The Ashkenazi Jews often treated the Arab Jews with disdain and discriminated against them in the political process, especially in the early incarnations of the Labor Party. Then, beginning in 1944 with the Zionist movement's "The Million Plan" (which will be discussed later), but especially after 1948 and the creation of Israel, hundreds of thousands of Arab Jews immigrated to Israel from the Middle East and North Africa. This influx, which was considered useful and encouraged since it increased the Jewish population, also increased these tensions between the different Jewish ethnicities. These tensions are still alive and well today in Israel with the Mizrahi and Sephardic Jews largely supporting the Likud party of Netanyahu and other right-of-center parties, while the Ashkenazi Jews largely support the Labor and left-of-center parties. Indeed, these strains had a big influence on the recent Israeli elections. This is actually ironic given the role the two groups played in the early formation of the state of Israel, but seems to be primarily a reaction against the Labor party. (This has some resemblance to the history of the loyalties of white Southerners in the U.S. regarding the Democratic and Republican parties.)

As to the numbers: The chart in **Appendix A** shows that in 1800 the Mizrahi and Sephardic Jews represented only about 2.5% of the population of Palestine, while 89.5% were Muslim and 8% were Christian. The best estimate is that the Jews numbered only about 7000. Almost all of the Christians were Palestinian Arabs following different branches of Christianity. So, while there indeed were Jews living in Palestine prior to the Zionist waves of immigration, more than 95% of the population was Palestinian. By 1890, the Jews of all ethnicities were about 8% (43,000). (We can thank the record keeping of the Ottoman Empire for what is believed to be quite accurate statistics.) By 1947, just before the creation of Israel, the entire Jewish population was 32.2% (about 630,000) out of the total population in Palestine of 1,964,000. (Here we can thank the British, who held the mandate over Palestine after the fall of the Ottoman Empire, for the stats.) Most of the increase in the Jewish population was Ashkenazi Jews who immigrated from Central and Eastern Europe.

Myth #3: The Zionist/Ashkenazi Jews Came to Palestine and Stole Land from the Palestinians Living There

This is a myth largely propagated by the Palestinians. The actual situation was more complicated. Prior to the fall of the Ottoman Empire (in 1919-1920 as a result of World Was I), most of the Palestinians who were farmers (many were shopkeepers and service workers in the cities), served as tenant farmers on land typically owned for generations by mostly non-Palestinian absentee landlords. These often lived in Damascus (the capital of the Ottoman province of Greater Syria) or in Constantinople/Istanbul. There were a few wealthy Palestinians living in Jerusalem, Jaffa or Hebron who also owned farm land. This was an established pattern and a poor Palestinian farming family would live and work on the same land for many generations (in some cases for hundreds of years) and understandably came to think of it as their own, even while paying rent to someone they rarely if ever saw.

Zionist Jews from Europe came to understand this system. As early as the late 1800s, they would identify a piece of land they wanted, then travel to Damascus or Constantinople and make a substantial offer in cash for the land. It was routinely accepted since no one else was likely to make such an offer and the owners felt no particular loyalty or obligation toward the Palestinian tenant farmers. The settler would then go to the Palestinian family living on the land, present the deed that had just been purchased, and inform the Palestinian family that they had to leave, usually immediately. If there was resistance, the Jewish settler would seek the support of the Ottoman authorities/police to evict the Palestinians. During the British Mandate (1920-1948), the same would be done, but it would be British soldiers or police who would enforce the purchase.

The Zionist movement raised money from Jews all over Europe and America to help "the poor Jewish settlers" buy some land to farm or on which to build a Kibbutz (a farming collective). The Jews contributing the money often had no idea that Palestinian families who had been living on the land for generations would not be receiving any of the money. Thus the displaced Palestinian family received no compensation at all, but suddenly lost their land, their home and their livelihood to a European Jewish settler. The Arab Jews had rarely done this, preferring for the most part to live in cities, and rarely having sufficient funds in any event. While these purchases from absentee landlords were typically done quite legally from a technical perspective, it felt like pure and simple thievery to the now homeless and destitute Palestinian family. Of course, there were exceptions to this pattern in that a wealthy Palestinian family living in Jaffa or Jerusalem would agree to sell some land to a Jewish settler or collective. But those doing this typically were severely criticized by the Palestinian community, so it was a relatively rare occurrence.

It was this expulsion of Palestinian tenant farmers from "their" land by Jewish settlers (Yishuv – literally: settler) that first stoked the hatred and anger of the Palestinians toward these Jewish settlers, especially toward the European (Ashkenazi) settlers. This is the origin of the Palestinian myth that the Jews came from Europe as colonialists and simply "stole" Palestinian lands; while the settlers sanctimoniously felt they had legally bought the property, albeit with no regard for the Palestinians who lived for generations on that land. To the Palestinian tenant farmers who received no compensation, it appeared as simple thievery. It is important to understand that it is this emerging conflict in the 1890's between Jewish Settlers and Palestinian tenant farmers that provides the foundation for what was to become the enduring Israeli-Palestinian conflict 50 years later.

Myth #4: Palestinians are Really Jordanians and have No Historical Sense of Palestinian Nationalism

As the Ottoman Empire collapsed and was dismantled by France and Britain (1919-1920), the ethnic Palestinians' sense of nationalism began to rise to the surface. Having been part of the Greater Syria Ottoman Province ruled from Damascus, groups of Palestinian leaders traveled there to petition to be allowed to establish a separate Palestinian state in all of what is now Jordan and what became the Palestinian Mandate area. However, since the Ottoman Empire was collapsing, the Syrians, who had no love for the Palestinians to begin with, also had no power to grant them anything. So this Palestinian effort was hopeless and bred anger and despair. But it was also the beginning of Palestinian Nationalism.

Then, in 1920, the French and British divided up Greater Syria. Initially the entire area that is now Jordan together with what is now Israel and the West Bank was assigned to the British as the Palestinian Mandate area. But in a 1922 White Paper (also called the Churchill White Paper), at the request of the British, that area was split with the land east of the Jordan River to be called Transjordan, under the nominal power of the Hashemite Emir, Abdullah (from a non-Palestinian family tracing it roots back to Mohammed). But it remained under British control. The area west of the Jordan River was henceforth called the Palestine Mandate area, under direct British administration. Transjordan constituted 76% of the territory and the White Paper specified that the Balfour Declaration (which will be discussed later) would **not** apply there – that is, Transjordan was to be off-limits to Jewish settlement. (However, British Mandate Administration encompassed both parts, and British Mandate currency was used in both. Transjordan was not granted independence by Britain until 1946, two years before the founding of the state of Israel.)

Syria itself was defined separately and given to the French, who also got Lebanon, while Iraq went to the British. No one asked the Palestinians or any of the Arab peoples what they wanted. For all practical purposes they were to become the subjects of the French or British, just as they had been subjects of the Ottoman Turks. The Palestinians were furious, but those in Transjordan living under the Muslim Emir, with a good deal of autonomy, were relatively peaceful. However those living west of the Jordan River, in the now more narrowly defined Palestinian Mandate area, immediately undertook efforts to drive the British out of Palestine in order to establish their own Palestinian state. Thus, while these Palestinians very much resented the encroachment on "their" land of the European Zionists, by the early 1920s they focused most of their anger on the British.

There were Palestinian revolts in the early 1920s and The Great Palestinian Revolt (as it became known) in 1936, both focused on the British Mandate forces. But in both cases, some of the Palestinian anger spilled over against the Jewish settlers and there were attacks upon them as well, with a good deal of death and destruction among the Jews. While the British fairly quickly and brutally put down these revolts, it immediately became clear to the Jewish settlers that they would need to arm themselves and train military forces for their own protection. It also became very clear that if they wished to consider the creation of a Jewish settler state of Israel within the Palestinian territory (a clear goal of the Zionist movement from the beginning in the 1890s), they would need to have substantial military power to take and hold the land. So, starting in the early 1920's, almost 30 years before the founding of the State of Israel, the Jewish settlers began to organize, train and arm a rather sophisticated military force, mostly in secret under the noses of the British Mandate authorities.

The point is that Palestinians are not Jordanians and have never ruled in Jordan. But it is the case that about half the population of Jordan is ethnically Palestinian, the rest being of Bedouin, Arab and other ethnicities, all ruled since the early 1920s by a Hashemite family. When one counts the Palestinian refugees who fled into Jordan in 1946-49, and again in 1967, most of whom still live in refugee camps and do not have Jordanian citizenship, more than 60% of the population in the area called Jordan are of Palestinian ethnicity. However, in 1970, during what came to be called Black September, there was a Palestinian led revolt against the Hashemite King that was brutally put down and the entire leadership of the Palestinians, together with thousands of their fighters and their families, were driven out of Jordan, most fleeing to Lebanon, some ending up in North Africa. To say, as some Israel leaders have, including Benjamin Netanyahu, that "Palestinians already have a state and it is called Jordan" is to misrepresent history and reality. (Netanyahu can be viewed making this statement as he participated in a public debate for which a video exists at http://www.quora.com/What-do-Israeli-conservatives-think-of-the-statement-Palestinians-already-have-a-state-its-called-Jordan)

Golda Meir, a former Prime Minister of Israel, was quoted on June 15, 1969 in the Sunday (London) Times saying:

> "There were (sic) no such thing as Palestinians...It was not as though there was a Palestinian people in Palestine considering itself a Palestinian people and we came and threw them out and took their country away from them. They did not exist."

In making this statement, she is demonstrating a willful blindness to the history of Palestinian nationalism and self-identity that goes back at least to the early 1920s.

The Balfour Declaration regarding the Establishment of a Jewish National Home in Palestine and
The Terms for the British Mandate over Palestine

It must be noted that during the mandate period, British authorities clearly favored the economic and social development of the Jewish settlers while merely preserving the civil and religious rights of the Palestinian Arabs. In part, this reflected a sense of responsibility for implementing the intent of the Balfour Declaration as specified in the terms the Council of the League of Nations set forth in establishing the British Mandate over Palestine. The **Balfour Declaration** (November 2, 1917) was a letter from the United Kingdom's Foreign Secretary Arthur James Balfour to Baron Walter Rothschild, a leader of the British Jewish community, for transmission to the Zionist Federation of Great Britain and Ireland. The exact words, in full, of this declaration are:

> "His Majesty's government view with favour the establishment in Palestine of a national home for the Jewish people, and will use their best endeavours to facilitate the achievement of this object, it being clearly understood that nothing shall be done which may prejudice the civil and religious rights of existing non-Jewish communities in Palestine, or the rights and political status enjoyed by Jews in any other country."

There has been much debate as to what was meant by the term "national home." To this point, Leopold Amery, one of the Secretaries to the British War Cabinet of 1917–18, testified under oath to the Anglo-American Committee of Inquiry in January 1946 from his personal knowledge that:

> "The phrase 'the establishment in Palestine of a National Home for the Jewish people' was intended and understood by all concerned to mean at the time of the Balfour Declaration that Palestine would ultimately become a 'Jewish Commonwealth' or a 'Jewish State', if only Jews came and settled there in sufficient numbers." (Quoted in Martinus Nijhoff, *The Palestine Yearbook of International Law,* 1984)

When the Council of the League of Nations established the terms under which Britain was to operate the mandate over Palestine, that document stated in part:

- "… the Principal Allied Powers have also agreed that the Mandatory should be responsible for putting into effect the declaration originally made on November 2nd, 1917… in favor of the establishment in Palestine of a national home for the Jewish people, it being clearly understood that nothing should be done which might prejudice the civil and religious rights of existing non-Jewish communities in Palestine." (Preamble)

- "The Mandatory shall be responsible for placing the country under such political, administrative and economic conditions as will secure the establishment of the Jewish national home and…the development of self-governing institutions, and also for safeguarding the civil and religious rights of all the inhabitants of Palestine, irrespective of race and religion." (Article 2)

- "An appropriate Jewish agency shall be recognised as a public body for the purpose of advising and co-operating with the Administration of Palestine in such economic, social and other matters as may affect the establishment of the Jewish national home and the interests of the Jewish population in Palestine." (Article 4)

- The Administration of Palestine, while ensuring that the rights and position of other sections of the population are not prejudiced, shall facilitate Jewish immigration under suitable conditions and shall encourage, in co-operation with the Jewish agency… close settlement by Jews on the land…" (Article 6)

- "The Administration of Palestine shall be responsible for enacting a nationality law. There shall be included in this law provisions framed so as to facilitate the acquisition of Palestinian citizenship by Jews who take up their permanent residence in Palestine." (Article 7)

Needless to say, the Palestinians were outraged that the British Mandate Authority seemed determined to carry out the intent of the Balfour Declaration by implementing the above terms set forth by the Council of the League of Nations in which they, the Palestinians, had no voice whatsoever. Thus, the British allowed, even encouraged, Jewish immigration (though this was done in a very inconsistent manner, depending on outside pressures, and stopped at the end of World War II). Another example was that as improvements in farming technology were developed in Britain, these were shared with the Jewish settlers, but not with the Palestinian farmers. Far better and more sophisticated schools were established for the Jewish settlers than for the Palestinians. The British often turned a relatively blind eye toward the effort of the Jewish settlers to develop and train military forces of their own, some of whom fought alongside the British in World War II (as will be discussed below). It soon became apparent to the Palestinians that the British Mandate Authority's sense of responsibility regarding the Jewish settlers and the establishment of a Jewish homeland took primacy over their responsibility to be even-handed. Hence, not surprisingly, the British became the prime enemy and the target of continued violence by Palestinians.

Myth #5: The Jews Living in Palestine Prior to World War II were Not Nationalists and They Were Willing to Live Peacefully with their Palestinian Neighbors.

As mentioned earlier, Sephardic Jews had been immigrating to Palestine since the 1500s, and there were some religious Eastern European (Ashkenazi) Jews who had immigrated to Palestine in the late 1700s and early 1800s – but neither of these groups, nor the Mizrahi Jews who were already there, sought to build a political state, an independent nation. In some cases this was consistent with elements of orthodox Jewish theology which held that a new Jewish state must await the coming of the Messiah. But starting in the late 1800s, the newly emerging Ashkenazi Zionist movement (which was not at all orthodox, in fact was often rather secular) clearly embraced the idea of eventually creating a nation state in Palestine (after having considered Argentina, East Africa and Far East Russia). This represented the initial rise of modern Jewish Nationalism, which matured and became a stronger ideology as the early Zionists saw the possibility of success in founding a state in Palestine following the issuance of the Balfour Declaration (1917), the collapse of the Ottoman Empire (1919-1920) and the increase in the Jewish population in Palestine from 13.6% in 1914 to 17.1% in 1931, to 32.2% in 1947. (Again, see chart in Appendix A)

Thus, tragically, these two nationalist movements emerged at the same time and in the same place. (Recall the earlier discussion concerning the rise of Palestinian nationalism in the discussion of the myth (# 4) that Palestinians are simply Jordanians.) Conflict became inevitable. But let's be clear: Palestinian nationalism was being expressed by a people whose direct forebears had lived and worked in that space for hundreds, even thousands of years, while the vast majority of the local proponents of Jewish nationalism were recent (less than 30-40 years) immigrants with little of their own family history in that space. Instead, these nationalistic Ashkenazi Jews based much of their claim on the prior presence of a small number (about 7,000 in 1800) Mizrahi and Sephardic Jews who indeed had also been there for hundreds, even thousands, of years. But those earlier Jewish residents had no nationalist plans. The Jewish nationalists, almost all Ashkenazi initially, also based their claim on the spirit of the Balfour Declaration, which the Palestinians viewed as an outright colonialist statement with no moral or legal standing that they recognized. Of course, years later, in the aftermath of the Holocaust in Europe, and in the face of the unwillingness of the developed nations of the world to offer sanctuary to Jewish refugees fleeing the Holocaust or to the Displaced Persons (DPs) who survived it in Europe, there was a general feeling of guilt and consternation. This led to a widespread view that a home for the Jews had to be found somewhere, just not in any of the developed nations. So why not support a Jewish Homeland in Palestine? That would relieve the guilt and solve the DP problem. But recall the statement quoted earlier by Ben-Gurion, the Zionist leader and first Prime Minister of Israel:

> "Sure, God promised it [Palestine] to us, but what does that matter to them [the Palestinians]? There has been anti-Semitism, Hitler, the Nazis, Auschwitz, but was that their fault? **They only see one thing: We have come here and stolen their country."** (Emphasis added.)

So, in the face of this history, the question must be asked: Who had the stronger moral claim to build a nation state in Palestine - the Jewish settlers or the Palestinians?

One possible answer to this question is to adopt the tactic of King Solomon when faced with two women who both claimed a child as her own – cut the baby in half. But as we turn to the next set of myths about the founding of the State of Israel and then about efforts to move toward a Two-State Solution, we see that, for the most part, neither side has been willing to divide the baby in a manner acceptable to the other. By the way, in the King Solomon story, one woman said: "Fine, cut it in half!," while the other cried out: "No, then she can have it!" In the bible story, King Solomon gave the baby to the woman who was willing to give it up rather than see it killed. I leave it to the reader to decide who is who in the Palestinian-Israeli situation.

Part II - Myths about The War* of Independence / *Al Nakba* (The Catastrophe) and about the Founding of the State of Israel

* Actually two wars: the Civil War (November 1947-May 1948) and the War of Independence (May 1948 – February 1949)

Myth #6 – Israel was Created by a Partition of Palestine as Mandated by the United Nations (In General Assembly Resolution #181)

This is perhaps the most pernicious of the myths we will address. To provide a brief historical overview: Britain, having tired of its role of operating the mandate over Palestine (due to the resistance to its rule by both Palestinians and Jewish settlers), declared in 1946 that it would abandon its mandate on Aug. 1st, 1948. (It actually did so on May 15, 1948, the day after Israel simply declared its independence.) Instead, it said it would turn over to the newly formed United Nations responsibility for deciding what to do next. A U.N. commission studied the matter, but could not come to a binding conclusion under the U.N.'s rules, and turned the matter over to the U.N. General Assembly. In 1947, following the growing awareness of the horrors of the Holocaust and the pictures of the waves of Displaced Persons (DPs) in camps throughout central Europe, European and American Jews and others, shocked by these images, appealed to the U.N. General Assembly for the creation of a Jewish Homeland in Palestine. While this was a heartfelt issue for American and European Jews who now supported the Zionist dream, it was a cynical effort by the leaders of many nations who had no more willingness to take in these DPs than they had had to take in Jews in the late 1930s and early 1940s when the Nazis were willing to let them go. (Just as many of these nations now resist allowing immigration from Syria and other war-torn nations.) So, with a combination of guilt and relief, there was broad support in the U.N. for creating two states, one Palestinian, one Jewish (with Jerusalem kept separate under international control). (An additional historical footnote: There had been earlier partition proposals going back to the Balfour Declaration (1917) (discussed above in some detail), the Peel Commission Partition Plan (1937), and the Woodward Palestine Partition Plans (1938) – but those are separate stories.)

The key point is that on Nov. 29, 1947, by a vote of 33 for, 13 against, and 10 abstentions (including, interestingly, the British), the U.N. General Assembly adopted Resolution # 181 *recommending* (and that is the essential word) to the Security Council the partition of Palestine, with 55.5% of the land to go to what was to be Israel and 44 .3% to Palestine (and about 0.2% for Jerusalem). This was at a point when the Jewish settlers accounted for just 32.2% of the population and owned or occupied only 7% of the land. Part of the Israeli portion was to include the Negev desert, which to the extent it was populated, it was by Bedouins. Certainly, from both a Palestinian perspective, and from a broader Arab perspective, this proposal was viewed as grossly unfair and inappropriate.

However, despite a series of proposals to the Security Council concerning this recommendation (some calling for modifications of it), it was **never approved or adopted** by that body. Here it is essential to cite the U.N. Charter:

> "Broadly speaking, while the General Assembly may discuss any international disputes or situations, **it is the Security Council** which recommends appropriate procedures or methods of adjustment or terms of settlement for the pacific settlement of disputes and takes preventive or enforcement measures with respect to threats to the peace, breaches of the peace or acts of aggression." (Emphasis added)

The Security Council never acted on the partition plan and never endorsed or accepted resolution # 181. Moreover, in January 1948 (four months before the Israeli declaration of independence), President Truman reversed the U.S. position and withdrew his support for the partition plan because of the heavy fighting that was already going on by that point in time. (The nature of this fighting will be discussed in a moment.)

To reinforce this point: Cambridge Professor, Sir Elihu Lauterpacht, Judge ad hoc of the International Court of Justice, and a renowned expert on international law, clarified, that from a legal standpoint, the 1947 U.N. General Assembly Resolution # 181 had no legislative character to vest territorial rights to either Jews or Arabs. He stated that:

"The coming into existence of Israel does not depend legally upon the Resolution. The right of a State to exist flows from its factual existence."

Reviewing Lauterpacht's arguments, another distinguished authority on the Law of Nations, Professor Stone of Oxford, added that Israel's "legitimacy" or the "legal foundation" for its birth does not reside with the United Nations' Partition Plan; instead he concluded:

"... The State of Israel is thus not legally derived from the partition plan, but rests (as do most other states in the world) on assertion of independence by its people and government, on the vindication of that independence by arms against assault by other states, and on the establishment of orderly government within territory under its stable control."

Let me be very clear. The point is not to challenge either the legitimacy of the State of Israel or its right to exist today. The point is that **Israel came into existence not by an act of the U.N. authorizing it, but by a unilateral decision by Jewish settlers living in Palestine to simply declare themselves to be a State** – very much as the American colonists in 1776 simply chose to declare their independence and their right to create a nation which they called the United States of America. But a critical difference needs to be acknowledged: unlike the Americans who declared their independence from a foreign nation, Britain, the Jewish settlers declared their right to form a state against the interests and very publicly stated desire of the overwhelming majority of the indigenous inhabitants of the area, the Palestinians. It would be akin to the American colonists declaring their independence and their state against the interests of the Native Americans, or of white European colonists in Africa declaring their right to create a state against the interests of the overwhelming majority of black inhabitants of those areas. In all of these cases, it was to be expected that the indigenous peoples would resist, usually by force, the creation of such a state on "their" territory.

That other established nations choose to recognize the legitimacy of the newly declared state, whether it be America in 1776 or Israel in 1948, and for practical purposes ratify its existence, does not for a moment provide the moral legitimacy that might have existed had the U.N. Security Council, with the approval of both the Jewish settlers and the Palestinians, declared the establishment of the states of Israel *and* Palestine (which indeed was the intent of Resolution 181). The Jewish settlers then, Israelis now, and Zionists around the world ever since 1947-48, should understand this distinction quite clearly. But they have chosen for almost 70 years to propagate a myth of moral legitimacy by claiming that the State of Israel was created by an act of the U.N. – when no such thing happened. To demand that this historical fact be acknowledged is not to be anti-Israel, and certainly not to be anti-Semitic, but to simply ask for historical honesty. Thinking back to the quotes from Paul Krugman about intellectual integrity, is this really such an unreasonable thing to ask for? Indeed, as Golda Meir put it in her book, *My Life,*

"One cannot and must not try to erase the past merely because it does not fit the present."

(See *also The Myth of the U.N. Creation of Israel*, Jeremy R. Hammond, *Foreign Policy Journal*, Oct. 26, 2010)

The Israeli War of Independence: 1947-49 (Actually, two wars: 1947-48 and 1948-49)

Let us turn from the issue of the legal basis for the declaration of Israeli independence to the controversies associated with the military conflicts of 1947-49. The Israelis refer to these conflicts as their War of Independence, out of which the borders of the State of Israel emerged in 1949. This conflict is referred to by the Palestinians as *Al Nakba* (The Catastrophe). According to the Israel Ministry of Foreign Affairs, the war was fought in four phases from November 30, 1947, the day after the Partition Resolution was approved by the U.N. General Assembly, until July 20, 1949, when Syria signed an armistice agreement. These 1949 borders lasted until the end of the Six Day War of 1967 and are often referred to as the 1967 Borders or The Green Line. There is general international agreement that these are the borders, with some reasonable land swaps, that must be the basis for any Two-State Solution.

It is certainly true that every nation has founding myths that help to define the national character and which often have strong, continuing effects on public attitudes and policies years later. In the Israeli case, there are five key myths associated with this period of conflict which need to be explored, not simply as a matter of historical accuracy or intellectual integrity, but because of the impact the belief in these myths has on the attitudes of Israeli and American Jews today. This is critical, because these attitudes directly affect the willingness to move toward an agreement to come to a Two-State Solution to the on-going conflict. And that's the point, without understanding that these are myths, that in a fundamental way they are **not** true, one has great difficulty overcoming their sway on **current** policies. I am convinced that unless and until both American and Israeli Jews understand the false basis upon which these myths stand, neither group will be prepared to reconsider their attitudes toward the founding of Israel, the nature of the Palestinian grievances, and the moral and legal basis for the need to move toward a Two-State Solution.

Before addressing these five myths directly, a few preliminary comments are necessary. This conflict includes a period of Civil War from November 30, 1947 to the Israeli Declaration of Independence on May 14, 1948, during which Jewish settlers and the military units they formed fought against the Palestinian inhabitants and their militias throughout the lands they shared – no outside Arab national forces were involved (although there were some Muslim volunteers who fought under the banner of the Arab Liberation Army – more about that below). The actual War of Independence began the day after the Declaration of Independence during which the settlers, who now became Israelis, fought against both Palestinian militias and elements of the armies of five nearby Arab nations that invaded the Palestinian mandate area. These wars were far and away the most costly in human terms that Israel has fought. Israel suffered 6,373 dead (about 1% of its population in 1947) and more than 15,000 wounded. Of the dead, about 4,000 were soldiers, the rest non-combatants. Almost one-third of the Israeli dead, about 2,000, were Holocaust survivors. There are major discrepancies as to the number of casualties among Palestinians and other Arabs. The estimated number of Arab dead ranges from a low of 3,700 to a high of 13,000. There is little argument that the vast majority of the Arabs killed were Palestinian, and that the overwhelming majority of them were non-combatants, as we will discuss below. The point that I want to make here is that there is no question that the people of Israel suffered major losses, that some of the battles were fierce, and that in some of these encounters the Arab forces had superior arms, though rarely superior numbers. The essential point is that to discuss and discredit the validity of these myths is not to take an anti-Israel position, nor to minimize the seriousness of the conflict. Instead, this discussion is necessary to call upon Israeli and American Jews to confront the fact that these myths are not true, so that all involved are able to go forward based upon a more accurate understanding of history and of the basis for the positions each side takes in the current negotiations.

What are these myths? I will list all five of them here, to put them all upon the table up front. I will then undertake a discussion that will address each of them, explaining why the myth is false or vastly overstated. Please note that what follows is in no way meant to be a complete description or analysis of this war. Many very detailed books have been written on that topic. Instead, I will focus on those aspects of the conflict that enable us to evaluate these myths.

Myth #7:   **The Jewish Settlers accepted the Partition Map of Palestine as recommended by the U.N. General Assembly, while the Palestinians (and other Arabs) did not.**

Myth #8:   **The Jewish Settlers were vastly outnumbered by the Palestinian militias and Arab invading forces, and the Settlers/Israelis suffered from a severe shortage of weapons.**

Myth #9:   **The armed conflict between the Jewish Settlers/Israelis and the Palestinians/Arabs began when the Armies of Five Arab Nations (Syria, Jordan, Iraq, Egypt and Lebanon) invaded Palestine on May 15, 1948, the day following the Israeli Declaration of Independence.**

Myth #10: **The Palestinians who fled their homes did so voluntarily to avoid the conflict or at the urging of their leaders. The charge that the Israelis engaged in systematic "ethnic cleansing" to drive the Palestinians out of territory the Israelis intended to occupy is without foundation.**

Myth #11: **Except for one regrettable incident (Deir Yassim), the charge that the Jewish military forces committed a whole series of massacres of unarmed men, women and children is not true. In fact, it was the Arabs who committed many such massacres.**

Re Myth # 7: Did either side accept the Partition Map recommended by the U.N. General Assembly?
The answer is an emphatic NO !

Let us begin by asking how did the Palestinians and the surrounding Arab states react to the U.N. General Assembly's decision to recommend the Partition Plan? In the case of the Palestinians and their leadership there was immediate despair, outrage and virtually total rejection, though one of the ruling Palestinian families indicated some modicum of support. Every one of the Arab states in the U.N. had voted against the resolution, arguing that it violated the founding principle of the U.N. Charter which called for self-determination of peoples. Instead, this resolution called for imposing what the Arabs, and in particular the Palestinians, felt was a totally unfair distribution of the land of Palestine and the establishment of a colonial state within Palestinian territory, one that would include more than 300,000 Palestinians and about 600,000 Jews. The Arab states indicated, even before the vote, that they would resist the implementation of this plan by force of arms if needed. Since the resolution required for its implementation that both sides accept the plan, when one side totally rejected it, the proposal became moot – which was part of why the Security Council never adopted it.

How did the Jewish settlers react? The answer here is much more complicated. Initially there was unbridled joy that their right to have a state had been acknowledged and that so much of the land would become theirs. Especially among the public, there seemed to be little understanding of the difference between what was simply a recommendation of the U.N. General Assembly and an actionable plan to implement the Partition by the Security Council. Officially and publicly, the Jewish Agency Executive, which was the informal governing body for the settlers, accepted the plan. But in fact, there is clear historical evidence that quietly most of the Jewish leadership was absolutely **unwilling** to accept the boundaries in the plan. They saw five problems:

1) The territory proposed to become Israel was divided into three separate parts by connections between the territories assigned to the Palestinians. (See Appendix E - Map of U.N. Partition Plan)
2) The territory to be Israel contained hundreds of Palestinian villages inhabited by more than 300,000 Palestinians, who, under the U.N. plan, would constitute fully one-third of the population of Israel.
3) The proposed Israeli territory did not contain the northern Galilee Valley area which the settlers considered essential.
4) Jerusalem was to be under international control and left deep within Palestinian territory with no route for the Israelis to have access to it.
5) The city of Jaffa was to be included in Palestine, even though it was a coastal enclave just south of Tel Aviv, and in the middle of an area to be part of Israel.

Having seen the proposed map weeks, even months, before the vote, the Jewish settler leadership immediately began to draw up military plans designed:

a) to consolidate control over all of their **assigned** territory (Recall that at the beginning the Jewish settlers only controlled 7% of the Palestine Mandate area, not the 55.5% of the land designated by the U.N. General Assembly recommendation to become Israel)
b) to gain access to and control over Jerusalem, without regard to the U.N. plans to place it under international stewardship
c) to seize control of the northern Galilee valley and to open a broad path between the coastal plain and the Negev (by taking control of the U.N. proposed Gaza strip which was to be included in Palestine per the U.N. plan), so as to ensure a contiguous national space
d) to seize control of Jaffa and its surrounding citrus groves
e) to remove most of the 300,000 Palestinians in the areas designated by U.N. General Assembly to be Israel, as well as the additional hundreds of thousands living in the Northern Galilee, in Jaffa, in the Gaza strip, and along the road to Jerusalem, which together would have constituted well over 50% of the population in the land they intended to be Israel. As we shall see below, more than 700,000 Palestinians left or were moved out of the territory that became Israel at the end of the wars.

On the last point, David Ben-Gurion had made his position clear years before: for example in 1938, when he stated in a speech before the Jewish Agency Executive: "I am for compulsory transfer: I do not see anything immoral in it." There is no dispute that Ben-Gurion advocated a policy of what we would now call "ethnic cleansing." The leadership of the Jewish Agency Executive, and especially Ben-Gurion and the military leaders, saw a fundamental contradiction between seizing a land area to be Israel only to find the Jewish settlers a minority within "their" new state. We will discuss this point in more detail shortly when we address Myths # 10 and 11 regarding how and why Palestinians left and the controversial issue of massacres. But for now, the key point is to understand the falseness of Myth # 7 – **neither side** was at all prepared to accept the borders recommended by the U.N .General Assembly.

Both the Jewish settlers and the Palestinians had sat by their radios listening as the U.N. General Assembly voted on the Partition Plan. As soon as the vote approving the recommendation of the partition plan was announced, the settlers poured out of their homes to celebrate that their dream to have their own state was approved, while the Palestinians sat stunned that this organization **in which they had no direct voice** had just approved taking more than half of their land away from them to give it to this minority of mostly recent immigrants. (Can one imagine how "White" Americans would react if the U.N. recommended giving, as a separate nation, more than half of the U.S. to the Hispanic minority?) Not surprisingly, the Palestinians poured out of their homes in fury. Within hours, conflicts between the two groups began, especially in the urban areas, and these all too often quickly turned violent.

Regarding Myth # 8 concerning the relative sizes of the military forces and the amount and quality of military equipment available to the Jewish settlers/Israelis, as compared to the strength of the Palestinian militias and the invading armies from five Arab nations

The facts and figures cited in this section come from a broad array of sources including those listed here. But the essential point is not exactly how many of what sort of arms, including aircraft and artillery, were acquired by the settler/Israel military, but rather to appreciate the overall extent of planning and weapons acquisition that was carried out. Also, this is not in any way to criticize this program – given the anticipated conflict, it was brilliantly conceived and executed, and was obviously prudent. The point is to gain an appreciation for the extent of this effort as compared to the mythology about the comparative weakness of these forces. Also, as noted in this section, there were extensive diplomatic contacts by the setters with the Arab nations involved, especially with Transjordan and Lebanon. The key point here is to recognize that these contacts did occur, that there was extensive communications/negotiations, and that these had a significant impact on the military conflict.

A series of works by the Israeli historian, Benny Morris, including *1948: The First Arab-Israeli War*, (2008); *Righteous Victims: A History of the Zionist-Arab Conflict, 1881–2001* (2001); *The Birth of the Palestinian Refugee Problem, 1947–1949* (1988); *The Birth of the Palestinian Refugee Problem Revisited* (2004). Works by Yoav Gelber, a Israeli historian at the University of Haifa: *Israeli-Jordanian Dialogue, 1948–1953: Cooperation, Conspiracy, or Collusion?* (2004); *Palestine 1948. War, Escape and the Emergence of the Palestinian Refugee Problem* (2006); *Jewish-Transjordanian Relations 1921–48: Alliance of Bars Sinister* (1997); Bregman, Ahron: *Israel's Wars: A History Since 1947* (2002). Debra Kamin: *How a Fake Kibbutz Was Built to Hide a Bullet Factory: Israel's pre-state underground militia knew it has to prepare for war once the British left , and it concocted a brilliant way of doing so without getting caught*, Haaretz, Apr 15, 2013. Martin Van Creveld: *Sword and the Olive: A Critical History of the Israeli Defense Force,* (2002). Israel Ministry of Foreign Affairs: *Israel's War of Independence (1947-1949).* Inari Karsh, Efraun Karsh: *Empires of the Sand: The Struggle for Mastery in the Middle East, 1789–1923* (1999). Spencer C. Tucker: *The Encyclopedia of the Arab-Israeli Conflict: A Political, Social, and Military History* (2008). Meir Zami: *'Bid' for Altalena: France's Covert Action in the 1948 War in Palestine*, (2010). John Laffin: *The Israeli Army in the Middle East Wars 1948-73.* Arnold Krammer: *The Forgotten Friendship - Israel and the Soviet Bloc, 1947–53* (1974). David Tal: *War in Palestine, 1948: Israeli and Arab Strategy and Diplomacy* (2003). John Kimche, David Kimche: *A Clash of Destinies: The Arab-Jewish War and the Founding of the State of Israel* (1960). Rabbi Elmer Berger: *Peace for Palestine: First Lost Opportunity* (1993)

The critical point to understand is that the Jewish settlers had been militarily preparing for this conflict since the early 1920s and had intensified those preparations in 1946-47, having developed well-trained military units, stockpiles of arms (some stored outside Palestine until the mandate ended and they could be imported), armament manufacturing facilities within Palestine, and careful plans for the mobilization of their population (all under the not-so-watchful eyes of the British mandate forces.) On the other hand, the Palestinians had only organized some informal militia units that were neither well-trained nor well-armed. Moreover, all of these militias were under the control of local village and city leaders; there was no central command structure at all.

According to the Israeli historian, Benny Morris, by the end of 1947 (5 months **before** the Declaration of Independence), the Palestinians "had a healthy and demoralizing respect for the Yishuv's military power" and most observers agreed that if it came to battle, the Palestinians knew that on their own they would lose. Instead, the Palestinians relied upon the expectation that the armies of the four surrounding Arab nations: Jordan, Syria, Egypt, and Lebanon, plus Iraq, would come to their defense, quickly defeat the Jewish settlers and return all of Palestine to the Palestinians. But the Palestinians were to be sadly disappointed in all regards. But before looking more carefully at the reactions of the Palestinians and the nearby Arab nations, we need to explore the extent and nature of the military preparations that had been made by the Jewish settlers.

Manpower: In November 1947, the Haganah was an underground paramilitary force that had existed as a highly organized, "national force." (The Jewish settlers thought of themselves as a Jewish nation, but one that did not "yet have" a State.) It had been growing and developing since the Palestinian riots of **1920–21**, and throughout the Palestinian riots of **1929**, the Great Palestinian Uprising of **1936–39**, and World War II. It had a mobile force, the HISH, which had 2,000 full-time fighters (men and women) and 10,000 reservists (all age between 18 and 25) and an elite unit, the Palmach composed of 2,100 fighters and 1,000 reservists. The reservists trained three or four days **a month** and went back to civilian life the rest of the time. These mobile forces could rely on a garrison force, the HIM (*Heil Mishmar*, lit. Guard Corps), composed of people aged over 25. The Yishuv's (Jewish settlers) total strength in November 1947 was around 35,000 with 15,000 to 18,000 fighters and a garrison force of roughly 20,000. There were also several thousand men and women who had served in the British Army in World War II who did not serve in any of the underground militias, but would provide valuable military experience/leadership during the war. The Yishuv had the additional forces of the Jewish Settlement Police, numbering some 12,000, the Gadna Youth Battalions, and the armed settlers. But few of these units had been trained by December 1947. On December 5, 1947 (just days after the U.N, General Assembly vote), conscription was instituted for all men and women aged between 17 and 25 and by the end of March, 21,000 had been conscripted. On 30 March, the call-up was extended to men and single women age 26 to 35. Five days later, a General Mobilization order was issued for all men under 40. (There was no formal conscription among the Palestinians, in part because they had not done the prior planning, had no effective centralized command structure, and because they had no time before they were attacked by the organized settler forces.)

By March 1948, 2 months **before** the declaration of independence, the Yishuv **had clear numerical superiority**, with 35,780 mobilized and deployed troops for the Haganah, plus 3,000 Stern and Irgun fighters (considered by the British as terrorists), and a few thousand armed settlers. Moreover, immediately following the Israeli declaration of independence, American and Canadian Jewish military pilots, who had previously been contacted and organized, came to fly for the Israelis, in the same spirit as their compatriots went to Britain to help defend that nation in the early days of World War II. (We will discuss the size and structure of the Palestinian and other Arab forces below.)

The Acquisition of Armaments: In 1946 (a year **before** the U.N. Partition vote), Ben-Gurion decided that the Yishuv would need to build a much stronger military presence before it declared independence and accordingly began a "massive, covert arms acquisition campaign in the West" (Benny Morris). Here it is important to note the dates. **The plan to declare independence preceded by a full year the vote in the U.N. General Assembly regarding the Partition recommendation.** It was predicated on the anticipation of the British abandoning the Mandate, not on action by the U.N. The Yishuv managed to clandestinely amass arms and military equipment abroad for transfer to Palestine once the British blockade was lifted. In the United States, Yishuv agents purchased three B-17 bombers, one of which bombed Cairo in July 1948, some C-46 transport planes, and dozens of half-tracks, which were repainted and defined as "agricultural equipment". In Western Europe, Haganah agents amassed fifty 65mm French mountain guns (artillery pieces), twelve 120mm mortars, ten H-35 light tanks, and a large number of half-tracks. By mid-May the Yishuv had purchased from Czechoslovakia 25 Avia S-199 fighters (an inferior version of the German Messerschmitt ME-109), 200 heavy machine guns, 5,021 light machine guns, 24,500 rifles, and 52 million rounds of ammunition, enough to equip all units, but with some shortage of heavy arms. The airborne arms smuggling missions from Czechoslovakia were codenamed Operation *Balak*. Once Israel declared its independence and the British ended their Mandate the next day, the flow of weapons into Israel accelerated from the stockpiles already amassed and from new sales, especially from France and Czechoslovakia, as well as from the open international arms markets. Money to buy these weapons was apparently not a problem, massive fundraising having gone on since the end of World War II. Other weapons came unofficially and through various channels from the departing British forces, while virtually no British weapons found their way into Palestinian hands.

Arms Production: The Yishuv also had "a relatively advanced **arms producing** capacity", that between October 1947 and July 1948 "produced 3 million 9 mm bullets, 150,000 Mills grenades, 16,000 submachine guns (Sten guns) and 210 three-inch (76 mm) mortars", along with a few "Davidka" mortars, which had been indigenously designed and produced. The latter were inaccurate but had a spectacularly loud explosion that demoralized the enemy. A large amount of the munitions used by the Israelis came from the Ayalon Institute, a clandestine bullet factory underneath kibbutz Ayalon, which produced about 2.5 million bullets for Sten guns. The munitions produced by the Ayalon Institute were said to have been the only supply that was not in shortage during the war. Locally-produced explosives were also plentiful. After the declaration of Israel's independence, these clandestine arms manufacturing operations no longer had to be concealed, and were moved above ground. All of the Haganah's weapons-manufacturing was centralized and later became Israel Military Industries.

The essential point to bear in mind is that the image of the Jewish settlers/early Israelis as being poorly armed, reliant only upon pistols and light hunting rifles and at the mercy of the Arab forces is a fantasy – the classic David with his slingshot against the Arab Goliath was **not** the situation. The settler/Israeli forces were vastly better armed, far more numerous, better trained, and with better command and control than the Palestinian militias, and, as it turned out, were also more than a match for the combined Arab forces that later joined the battle. Israel's victory, while hard fought at times, was no fluke, no accident of history. It did not require "divine intervention" as some religious Jews would like to believe.

Myth # 9: A Two Stage War- first with the Palestinians and only later with the national Arab forces.
As the civil war began, all five of the afore mentioned Arab nations decided that they would **not** intervene so long as the British maintained their Mandate over Palestine. They were simply not prepared to enter into a battle with British forces in order to protect the Palestinians from Jewish settlers whom they considered to be of little military consequence. (There was one exception to this, which was the so-called Arab Liberation Army that was organized by Syria, which we will discuss in a moment.) So from November 30, 1947 (the day after the Partition Plan was voted upon) until May 15, 1948, when the British ended their mandate and began to withdraw from Palestine, the Jewish settlers' forces had a totally dominant military position, even when one includes the forces fighting under the banner of the Arab Liberation Army. Sadly for the Palestinians, the British forces chose not to seriously intervene to protect the Palestinians from the Jewish settlers' well-trained and well-armed forces. But neither did the British protect the Jewish settlers from the marauding Palestinians gangs and militias. In those first few days and weeks, many Jewish settlers were killed and hurt. But also within a few days, the well-trained Haganah forces, the elite Palmach forces (many of whom had fought with the British in World War II), and the Irgun and Stern Gangs (who were labeled as terrorists by the British) all emerged, and the tide of battle immediately swept to the Jewish side.

As the Palestinians had feared, their militias were rather quickly marginalized. Indeed, before the end of March (two months **before** the Israeli Declaration of Independence), a well-organized, carefully planned program of ethnic cleansing under the terms of Plan *Dalet* began. This will be discussed below in regard to Myths # 10 and 11 concerning why the Palestinians left and whether there were massacres. The fact is that the Jewish settlers had by April 1948 already taken control over virtually all of the territory identified in the U.N. Partition recommendation (increasing their control from 7% of the land in November 1947 to 56% in April/May 1948) and had even begun to take control of additional Palestinian designated land – all well before the Declaration of Independence and the intersession of the Arab nations. Moreover, by May 1948, most of the Palestinians who had lived in those areas were gone.

The Invasion by the Five Arab Armies

On May 15, 1948, the day after Israel declared independence and the day the British mandate ended, the Five Arab nations named above began their attacks inside Palestine. But simply stating that fact totally fails to adequately provide a sense of what occurred. To be sure, the combined population of these five Arab nations was many times that of the Jewish settlers, and the Arab standing armies were far larger than those of the Jewish settlers. But none of these Arab nations took any steps whatsoever to mobilize their populations and, for a variety of reasons, none of them committed a major proportion of their military forces to the attack in the Palestinian territory. Those who simply state and restate that the war pitted the Jewish settlers against five Arab nations are creating, often intentionally I would argue, a very misleading sense of the conflict. Moreover, while some in these Arab countries were making very inflammatory and threatening speeches as to the Arabs' goals (such as threats about killing all the Jews and/or driving them all into the sea), the official positions were more moderate, calling for the establishment of a single Palestinian state, with respect for Jewish minority rights within it. Nevertheless, the clear fact is that on the Jewish settlers' side, they had good reason to fear what was about to happen, to think that they did indeed face a threat, not only to their desire to claim a state for themselves, but a threat to their very existence. But it turned out that the forces that would be thrown against them were nowhere near as powerful as the Israelis feared. On the other hand, the Arab forces had totally underestimated the trained military and command skills of the Jewish settlers, the amount of weaponry they had marshaled, and the number of fighters they could assemble. To understand what actually did happen, it is essential to look at the role of each of the five Arab nations separately.

The Role of Transjordan (which became an independent kingdom in March 1946, renamed Jordan in 1948/49

The by-far best trained military force was Jordan's Arab Legion, which had been trained, armed and led by the British. During the months between November 1947 and May 1948, representatives of the King of Transjordan met with civilian and military leaders of the Jewish settlers (including Golda Meir). The King made it clear that his primary goal was to secure control over Jerusalem and the so-called West Bank (of the Jordan River). He made it quite clear that (a) he did not intend to allow an independent Palestinian state to emerge, (b) he was determined to incorporate at least the West Bank into Jordan, and (c) he was dedicated to bringing Jerusalem, especially the Old City, under Arab /Muslim/Jordanian control, no matter what the U.N. had planned for these areas. He would have preferred to take over all of Palestine, but apparently recognized the reality that he did not have sufficient military strength to defeat the emerging Israeli forces. So he entered into an agreement with the Jewish leadership that Jordan would enter Palestine with the goal of occupying the West Bank, including Jerusalem, but that Transjordanian forces would **not** engage with Israeli forces within the Israeli areas of the Partition Plan. That deal was largely sustained, except when the Israelis drove through the West Bank toward Jerusalem with the intent of taking control of the Old City. Jordan then moved to block and engage as necessary the Israelis and did succeed in retaining the Old City (and East Jerusalem) under Arab control. One interesting footnote was then when Jordan took control over the Old City, there were thousands of Jews living in the so-called Jewish Quarter, who were immediately set upon by angry mobs of Palestinians. The Arab Legion of Transjordan stepped in **to protect the Jews**, even killing a few Palestinians in the process, and then escorted these Jews out of the Old City into the hands of the Israeli forces moving into West Jerusalem. The only real military encounters between the Transjordanian Arab Legion and the Israelis occurred when Israel moved far beyond the Partition Plan boundaries, especially when it attempted to move toward and capture Jerusalem, thus violating the agreement that had been made with Transjordan's King. Transjordan failed in achieving one of its goals, which was to secure a path to the Mediterranean Sea through the West Bank and then through the northern tip of Gaza, because the Israelis took control over northern Gaza. This goal had not been communicated to the Israelis. Jordan committed 8,000 to 10,000 troops to this invasion across the Jordan River onto the West Bank.

The Role of Syria and the Arab Liberation Army

In 1948, Syria's Ba'ath Party leaders did not consider the regular army to be a reliable force, especially if deployed out of the country. It should be noted that Syria did not exist as an independent nation until 1944 and the French troops did not leave until April 1946. However, Syria did create the Arab Liberation Army (ALA) of volunteers from various Arab and non-Arab countries.   Since the ALA was not formally a Syrian force, they could risk sending it into Palestine before the British Mandate ended. There it joined with the Palestinian militias for a couple of months in the north in early 1948 and later fought elsewhere. The big impact of the ALA was that it had mortars and machine guns, which the Palestinian militias lacked. Most historians put this force at about 3500, though some claim it grew to as many as 6000 to 8000. Syria initially chose to maintain most of their own troops within Syria to defend against an attack from either Transjordan or Israel. However, in May 1948, Syria did commit about 2,500 troops (some claim as many as 5,000) in the north, including a small unit of tanks and some artillery and captured the Israeli village of Tzemah (one of a very few Israeli villages to fall). However, after being defeated in another nearby battle, a few days later they the abandoned Tzemah. In June, they succeeded in taking a second village, Mishmar HaYarden, but then assumed a defensive position except for "a few minor attacks on some small, exposed Israel settlements." (Morris) After that these troops were employed primarily by Syria as an unsuccessful blocking force to try to keep Jordan from gaining control of the West Bank. Syria did succeed in two of its military goals, retaining control of the strategic Golan Heights and of a portion of the east coastline of the Sea of Galilee (Lake Tiberius).

The Role of Lebanon

Lebanon really did not want to get into this war at all. But under pressure from other Arab nations they committed a small force, estimated at 800-1000, which engaged in a couple of short battles in the far north and then withdrew back to Lebanon. Israel then invaded and held territory in southern Lebanon until the end of the war. There are reports that Ben Gurion in June 1947 (five months **before** the U.N. vote on partition) "arrived at an agreement with the Maronite religious leadership in Lebanon that cost a few thousand pounds and kept Lebanon's army (that consisted of only about 3500) out of the War of Independence and the military Arab coalition." (Morris)

The Role of Iraq

Initially Iraq committed only about 3000 troops, but that increased to about 15,000, including one armored battalion. The key point is that the Iraq forces were put under Transjordanian command and fought exclusively within the West Bank. For example, they helped to repulse an Israeli attack on the Palestinian city of Jenin (deep within the West Bank area), but only after suffering heavy losses. By June 1948, just two months into the war "Active Iraqi involvement effectively ended." (Morris)

The Role of Egypt

Egypt committed by far the most military forces of any Arab nation. At its peak, they had 20,000 in the field, including tanks, artillery and some aircraft. But the key to understanding the Egyptian role is that their primary political/strategic goal was to secure their northeastern border between the Sinai (Egyptian) and the Negev (which the Partition plan assigned to Israel) areas, which including gaining control over the Gaza region. While there was talk of helping to establish a Palestinian state; in fact, it seemed to most observers that Egypt's primary goal was to maintain control over the Palestinians living near their borders and to prevent having a direct border with the emerging Israeli state. To this end, there were a number of pitched battles between the Israeli and Egyptian forces, all in the south of Palestine, with heavy casualties on both sides. The Egyptian forces had the heaviest weapons and had some air support. But the Israelis also deployed air power and some heavy weapons. In the end, the Israeli forces succeeded in establishing air superiority, even bombing Cairo, while Egypt never carried out any air raids beyond Gaza. Israel took control of almost 75% of the Gaza-strip designated by the U.N. plan to go to Palestine. Egypt retained control over about 25%, but most of that was along the Mediterranean coast, not along the border area with Sinai. Egypt was forced to cede most of its Sinai border to being next to Israeli controlled land. (See Appendix F for a map that shows these results.)

The Impact of Centralized Command and Control

The Jewish settlers/Israelis developed and exercised a very professional and centralized military command and control structure that enabled them to shift units and equipment to where it was needed. They even managed to compel the Irgun and Stern gangs to come under central military control. The five Arab armies, the Palestinian militias, and the Arab Liberation Army, despite a few token attempts, never exercised any serious degree of centralized command and control. They sometimes worked against each other's interest, and they were never able to shift forces to where they were needed. So while the Israelis did have to fight on multiple fronts simultaneously, they did so with internal lines of supply and control. Some of the Arab forces had short lines of control and supply (Transjordan), some were quite extended (Egypt, Iraq), but they could not shift supplies between different forces. In this regard, the Israeli forces were far superior and more effective.

The Balance of Forces during the War

The effective number of Palestinian combatants is listed at 12,000 by some historians while others calculate an initial Arab strength of approximately 23,500 troops, including the Syrian sponsored Arab Liberation Army. The total Arab forces, including those committed from the five Arab nations, is estimated at 49,000 in April, 1949 with some estimates of a peak strength of 51,000 to perhaps 63,000. On the other hand, the Jewish settler forces numbered about 35,000 in November 1947 when hostilities broke out. That number increased quickly to about 63,000, and reached a peak of 117,500 before the end of the war. This means that that the Yishuv/Israeli military forces outnumbered the Palestinians by 3 to 2, if not 3 to 1 in the early days of the war and, even after the interventions by the five Arab nations, never fell below a ratio of about 2 to 1 in Israel's favor.

The Outcome of the 1947-1949 Wars

Having demonstrated overwhelming military superiority, even achieving air superiority, over both the Palestinian and external Arab forces, Israel was the clear winner of the 1947-49 wars. See the map in Appendix F. Recall that the U.N. General Assembly's Partition Plan recommended allocating 55.5% of British Mandate Palestine to Israel and 44.3% to Palestine (with 0.2% to an internationalized Jerusalem). As a result of the civil war with the Palestinians that began the day after the U.N. vote on November 29, 1947, the Jewish settlers secured somewhat more than that 55.5% of the land by late April 1948, well **before** Israel declared its independence and the actual War of Independence began. By the time that latter war officially ended in July 1949, Israel controlled more than 77% of Palestine. For the Palestinians, the results were even more tragic than that number suggests – for they controlled **0.0%** of Palestine -- **none**. In fact, to the anger and horror of the Palestinians, not one of the five invading Arab nations had had any interest whatsoever in helping to foster an independent Palestinian state. Transjordan succeeded in capturing and retaining what was left of the West Bank, including the Old City of Jerusalem and East Jerusalem and incorporating that territory within Jordan (the name having been changed from TransJordan). Similarly, Egypt succeeded in capturing and retaining less than one-fourth of the Gaza area that the U.N. had allocated for the Palestinians, the rest having been captured by Israel. Looking at the Palestinian population in 1949 at the end of the war: 12% (156,000) were in Israel (but often as internal refugees away from their original homes and villages), 29.5% (383,000) were on the West Bank or in Gaza, and 54.7% (711,000) were refugees in UN-run camps outside Palestine. The rest had left the area and were refugees elsewhere. (See the figures at the bottom of the chart in Appendix A) The war was an unmitigated disaster for the Palestinians in every regard. Their subsequent bitterness and anger is hardly surprising.

Addressing Myths 10 & 11: The Issues of Ethnic Cleansing and of the Massacres of Non-Combatants

These two topics are perhaps the most sensitive and difficult for Jewish Israelis and American Jews to discuss. The typical response one gets when raising either topic is denial. The traditional story that one hears is that the Palestinians left their homes and left the territory that was becoming Israel either at the urging of their own leaders or simply out of the usual fear shown by refugees fleeing any conflict area. But most Jews will tell you there was no organized effort by the Jewish settlers or the Israeli forces to intentionally drive Palestinians out, there was not a program of ethnic cleansing. After all, that would be a war crime and would provide the Palestinian refugees a strong moral basis to claim the "right of return" – expressed, if not in being actually allowed to return to their home areas in Israel, by at least being entitled to an apology and compensation. But, in fact, there was a well-organized and implemented program of ethnic cleansing, and the evidence of this is irrefutable – being well-documented in military and government records released in 1999 under Israel's Freedom of Information Act fifty years after the war. Moreover, this has been widely written about by Jewish Israeli 'New Historians' based upon these records which include the names of which units were assigned to which Palestinian villages, the names of the commanders involved, and in some case even include motion pictures of the attacks and of the Palestinians being "escorted" away.

Similarly, Jewish Israelis and American Jews have a very difficult time discussing the issue of whether there was a series of massacres of Palestinian non-combatant men, women and children, both during the early civil war period and then during the war of independence. But these, too, occurred, and again are well-documented and written about by historians. In fact, there is evidence that some of the massacres were part of the ethnic cleansing, intended to instill such fear as word of them spread, that other Palestinians would flee simply upon the approach of settler/Israeli forces. Other massacres were apparently the result of a lack of discipline combined with anger and a desire for revenge. But regardless of the reasons, a substantial number of massacres of Palestinians did occur.

What is essential to understand is that sustaining the myths is not simply a matter of wanting to avoid distasteful subjects. Nor does it stem merely from of a desire to sustain the image of the heroic Jewish settlers and Israeli military forces as part of a positive narrative of the history of the founding of Israel. Much more is involved that is of **current** political importance. If one admits to the ethnic cleansing and the massacres, then that would justify the term used by the Palestinians, *Al Nakba*, The Catastrophe, and provide a very different moral and legal basis for their claims to land and/or compensation. So let us look at the evidence supporting the above statements.

The Ethnic Cleansing of Palestinians from Israeli Controlled Palestine/Israel

Ilan Pappe has been called "Israel's bravest, most principled, and most incisive historian." He has also been called "one of the world's sloppiest historians" by another Israeli historian, Benny Morris, Professor of History in the Middle East Studies Department in Ben Gurion University of the Negev in Be'er Sheva. Morris accuses Pappe of not paying sufficient attention to the fears and the context that motivated the actions of the settlers/Israelis. But he does not dispute Pappe's descriptions of their actions. Pappe, after holding positions at the University of Haifa and at the Emil Touma Institute for Palestinian and Israeli Studies in Haifa, moved to the University of Exeter in the U.K., where he directs the European Center for Palestine Studies and the Centre for Ethno-Political Studies. Some Israeli and American Jews consider him a traitor to Israel for his writings and speeches, and challenge his scholarship in an attempt to discredit him. In this regard, I am reminded of the words of Amos Oz, the famous Israeli writer and peace activist, who was quoted in the L.A. Times on May 9, 2015 as saying: "I regard the title traitor as an honorary declaration, and I wear it [as a] badge because I am in excellent company." He then mentioned Lincoln, the Prophet Jeremiah, many writers and intellectuals. Oz went on to say; "It may be a more respectable club that those who have never been called traitors by anyone." I suspect Pappe would quite agree with these sentiments.

> For a very mixed series of reviews of Pappe's book, *The Ethnic Cleansing of Palestine* (One World Publications, Oxford, 2006) see: Uri Ram, Middle East Journal, vol 62, (1), 2008; Jorgen Jensehaugen, Journal of Peace Research, vol 45, (1) 2008; Epraim Nimni, Journal of Palestine

Studies, vol 39 (3), 2010; Seth Frantzman, Middle East Quarterly, Spring 2008; Ian Black, The Guardian, Feb 17, 2007; Benny Morris, The New Republic, Mar. 17, 2011.

The following quotations are from Pappe's book:

"...on a cold Wednesday afternoon, 10 March 1948, a group of eleven men, veteran Zionist leaders together with young military Jewish officers, put the final touches on a plan for the ethnic cleansing of Palestine. That same evening, military orders were dispatched to the units on the ground to prepare for the systemic expulsion of the Palestinians from vast areas of the country. The orders came with a detailed description of the methods to be employed to forcibly evict the people: large-scale intimidation; laying siege to and bombarding villages and population centres; setting fire to homes, properties and goods; expulsion; demolition; and finally planting mines among the rubble to prevent any of the expelled inhabitants from returning. Each unit was issued with its own list of villages and neighborhoods as the targets of this master plan Codenamed Plan D (*Dalet* in Hebrew) [the fourth letter in the Hebrew alphabet], this was the fourth and final version of (earlier) less substantial plans that outlined the fate the Zionists had in store for Palestine and consequently for its native population...how the Zionist leadership contemplated dealing with the presence of so many Palestinians living in the land the Jewish national movement coveted as its own...the Palestinians had to go...The aim of the plan was in fact the destruction of both the rural and urban areas of Palestine."

Pappe goes on to quote another Jewish historian, Simcha Flapan, who observed that

"The military campaign against the Arabs, including the 'conquest and destruction of the rural areas, was set forth in the Hagana's Plan *Dalet*"

Pappe then argues that

"Clashes with local Palestinian militias provided the perfect context and pretext for implementing the ideological vision of an ethnically cleansed Palestine...Once the decision was taken, it took six months to complete the mission."

The six months being from March to September 1948 – note the campaign started 3 months **before** Israel declared its independence and was completed in the face of the later presence of the armies of the five nearby Arab nations.

Pappe concludes that:

"When it was over, more than half of Palestine's native population, close to 800,000 people, had been uprooted, 531 villages had been destroyed, and eleven urban neighborhoods emptied of their inhabitants [including in Jaffa which went from around 70,000 to only about 3,000 Palestinians]. The plan decided upon on 10 March 1948, and above all its systematic implementation in the following months, was a **clear-cut case of an ethnic cleansing operation, regarded under international law today as a crime against humanity**." (Emphasis added)

The key point to understand is that while Pappe's critics, including Morris, argue that the emerging conflict and the fears it engendered led to the ethnic cleansing, and while they attempt to paint a more charitable picture of the motivations of the settlers/Israelis, they do not, indeed cannot, dispute the fact that hundreds of thousands of Palestinians were compelled to leave hundreds of villages and urban neighborhoods. Nor can it be disputed that many of these villages were intentionally demolished even as their inhabitants fled so that they would understand that there was nothing left to which they could return. Most of the other emptied Palestinian villages and neighborhoods were quickly renamed with Hebrew designations and setters were moved in to occupy them.

The Issue of Massacres

One of the most profound issues associated with the wars of 1947-49 is the massacres that occurred. While most Israeli and American Jews who know anything about this topic will concede that Jewish forces killed about 100 unarmed men, women and children in the Palestinian village of *Deir Yassin*, the myth is that this was a sad and regrettable, but isolated incident and that it is blown out of all proportions by the critics of Israel and by the supporters of the Palestinians. Tragically, this is absolutely not true.

> For analysis by the Israeli historian Benny Morris see his *Birth of the Palestinian Refugee Problem Revisited*, Cambridge University Press 2004 and *1948: A History of the First Arab-Israeli War*, Yale University Press, 2008. See also Rosemarie Esber, *Under the Cover of War – The Zionist Expulsion of the Palestinians*, Arabicus Books, 2009, Saleh Abdekl Jawad, *"Zionist Massacres: The Creation of the Palestinian Refugee Problem in the 1948 War,"* in Benvenist et al, *Israel and the Palestinian Refugees*, Spring, 2007

Depending on the definition used, between 10 and 70 massacres occurred during the 1947-1949 wars. Yishuv (Jewish settlers) and later Israeli soldiers intentionally killed roughly 800 Arab civilians and prisoners of war. Most of these killings occurred as villages were overrun and captured during the second phase of the Civil War, during Operation *Dani*, *Operation Hiram* and Operation *Yoav* and during the implementation of Plan *Dalet* discussed above.

According to Benny Morris, Jewish forces were responsible for 24 massacres during the war. Aryeh Yizthaki attests to 10 major massacres with more than 50 victims each. Palestinian researcher Salman Abu-Sitta records 33, half of them occurring during the civil war period (1947-48). Saleh Abdel Jawad has listed 68 villages where acts of indiscriminate killing of prisoners, and civilians took place, even though there was no threat to Yishuv or Israeli soldiers.

According to Morris, the "worst cases" were the *Saliha* massacre with 60 to 70 killed, the *Deir Yassin* massacre with around 100, *Lydda* massacre with around 250 and the *Abu Shusha* massacre with 60-70. In the village of *al-Dawayima*, accounts of the death toll vary. Saleh Abd al-Jawad reports 100-200 casualties. Morris has estimated "hundreds" and also reports about the IDF investigation which concluded 100 villagers had been killed. David Ben-Gurion gave the figure of 70-80. Saleh Abd al-Jawad reports the village *Mukhtar's* account that 455 people were missing following the *al-Dawayima* massacre, including 170 women and children.

There were also massacres of Jewish settlers – but the records indicate "only" three. The known massacres of Jewish civilians were the Haifa Oil Refinery massacre where 39 Jews were killed by Arab workers after Irgun members had thrown a bomb into a crowd of Palestinians, and the *Kfar Etzion* massacre where around 120-150 surrendering defenders were killed by Arab irregulars, with the participation of Arab Legion soldiers. With 80 deaths, the attack on the Hadassah medical convoy on the road to Jerusalem is also reported as a massacre because it included the mass killing of unarmed medical personnel by Arabs. There were other instances of unarmed Jewish settlers being killed by Palestinian militias and rioting crowds during the early days of the conflict.

Causes of the Massacres
 The causes of the massacres of Palestinians are a matter of controversy. Morris considers that the killings and massacres occurred "[l]ike [in] most wars involving built-up areas." Other historians talk of the anger and desire for revenge after Palestinian militias killed unarmed setters in various riots during the very early days of the conflict. According to Pappe, many of these massacres took place in the context of an ethnic cleansing campaign (as part of Plan *Dalet* and earlier related operations) that "carr[ied] with it atrocious acts of mass killing and butchering of thousands of Palestinians. They were killed ruthlessly and savagely by Israeli troops of all backgrounds, ranks and ages." Note that Pappe refers to "thousands," whereas most others put the number around 800. But ultimately, the issue is not the exact number of civilians intentionally killed, but rather the fact that there clearly were 10 to 70 significant incidents that historians agree occurred. This was more than enough for word of such massacres to spread quickly and widely.

During the civil war, the Haganah operatives had been cautioned against harming women and children but the Irgun and Stern groups did not observe this distinction, while "Palestinian Arab militias often deliberately targeted civilians." Due to the fact that the British Mandate was not yet over, neither side could set up regular prisoner of war camps during the civil war period and therefore took very few prisoners. Instead those defeated by either side were mostly driven to retreat and flee, or were killed. During the Arab-Israeli war following Israel's Declaration of Independence, the fighting armies were more or less disciplined and "the killings of civilians and prisoners of war almost stopped, except for the series of atrocities committed by the IDF forces" (Morris).

Despite their rhetoric, Arab armies committed few atrocities and no large-scale massacre of prisoners took place when circumstances might have allowed for that to happen, as when they took the Old City of Jerusalem with its Jewish Quarter or the villages of *Atarot, Neve Yaakov, Nitzanim, Gezer* and *Mishmar Hayarden*. On the contrary, on 28 May, when the Jewish inhabitants and fighters of the Old City surrendered and feared for their lives, the Transjordanian Arab Legion protected them from the mob and even wounded or shot dead other Arabs in doing so.

With regard to massacres perpetrated by the IDF toward the end of the war and particularly during Operation Hiram, where around 10 massacres occurred, Morris and Yoav Gelber (another Israeli historian) consider that lack of discipline **cannot** explain the events. Gelber points out the "hard feelings [of the soldiers] towards the Palestinians" and the fact that "the Palestinians had not fled like in former operations." Benny Morris thinks that they were related to a "general vengefulness and a desire by local commanders to precipitate a civilian exodus" [ethnic cleansing].

To explain the difference in the number of killings and massacres committed by the settlers/Israelis compared to those committed by the Palestinian and other Arab forces, Morris speculates that "[t]his was probably due to the circumstance that the victorious Israelis captured some four hundred Arab villages and towns during April–November 1948, whereas the Palestinian Arabs and the Arab Liberation Army failed to take any settlements and the Arab armies that invaded in mid-May overran fewer than a dozen Jewish settlements".

For the purposes of this paper, it is critical that the reader not get caught up in the disputes over the exact number of massacres or the exact number of innocent civilians intentionally killed by either side. Moreover, for the purposes of this paper, the focus is not upon an examination of what the motivations for the massacres by the Jewish settler/Israeli forces might have been. These are interesting and important issues, but are not the focus here. The key point that is the focus of concern of this paper is that before Israeli or American Jews can discuss **why** the ethnic cleansing and massacres happened, one must first acknowledge that they indeed **did happen**, and that the myths to the contrary are false. And this acknowledgement has not happened broadly within either the Israeli or American Jewish communities, despite the many books and articles on the subject, including articles in the Israeli popular press.

Here it is relevant to consider the comments by Benny Morris, as quoted in an interview published in *The Middle East Quarterly* (Summer 2010, volume 17, number 3)

> "There are historians who are always preoccupied with concealing things, but I always have believed it is important to teach the truth. Many people are deterred from publishing things of this sort because they believe this will undermine self-confidence and the feeling of justice inherent in Zionism, and if we lose this feeling of justice, it will weaken us. I don't think this is correct. It is more important for people to know the truth, and if this causes them to be a little unsure in their self-justification—so let them be a little unsure."

It should be noted that, as reported in that same article cited just above, Morris secured the professorship at Ben Gurion University of the Negev in large part due to the intervention of Ezer Weizman, who, when President of Israel, felt he had to personally intervene to secure that position for Morris who was being hounded out of academia, indeed out of Israel, for his academic work. Similarly, Pappe (who was far more politically engaged than Morris) was forced to flee Israel after multiple threats to his life, including having his picture printed on the front page of a newspaper over the image of a target. It should be noted that Morris and Pappe are fierce critics of each other's work. But while they harshly critique each other's tone and interpretations of the motivations and intent of the Israeli forces, they ultimately reinforce most of each other's statements of the actual facts on the ground.

The Combined Impact of the Ethnic Cleansing and the Massacres

When one considers why more than 700,000 Palestinians fled their homes and villages, one must understand that this was more than the usual stream of refugees who always flee conflict areas, although some surely fit that description. But in the case of the wars of 1947-49, it was far more than that. Aside from directly suffering from the program of ethnic cleansing, many, perhaps most, of these people knew of the massacres and fled (or allowed themselves to be docilely "escorted" away) out of a **well-founded** abject fear of being murdered if they did not. In light of this history, is it any wonder that the descendants of these Palestinian refugees retain intense, self-righteous anger about what happened to their grandparents and parents and harbor an intense desire to return to the homes and villages in which their families had lived for generations? The fact that these villages and homes typically do not even exist today, and that such a return is politically impossible, only increases their frustration and pain and anger.

The Public Availability Today of Detailed Information about the Palestinian Villages that Existed Prior to 1947

It is important to be aware that in Israel the fact that most Israeli towns are literally built upon the ruins of Palestinian villages (recall the statement to this effect by Moshe Dayan cited earlier) is something that is available information for anyone willing to seek it. For example, there are books, even tour books, maps and even phone apps that, based upon careful research, show the locations of these Palestinian villages. These books and maps have been reviewed and discussed in the Israeli press. The leading group publishing this material is Zochrot (which is Hebrew and translates as 'remembering'). Zochrot is an Israeli NGO founded in 2002 in Tel Aviv. Its founding director is Eitan Bronstein and the current director is Liat Rosenberg, both are Jewish Israelis. Its slogan is: "To commemorate, witness, acknowledge and repair." Quoting from their website:

> "Zochrot and other Israeli NGOs have been fairly successful over the past few years in raising the Nakba to the awareness of the broad Jewish public. The destruction of hundreds of villages and resulting hundreds of thousands of Palestinian refugees in the 1948 War have become part and parcel of current Israeli discourse; nevertheless, its mere presence in Jewish Israeli discourse still does not mean broad acknowledgement of and accountability for the Nakba. This gap is largely due to the continued adherence of Jewish Israeli society to colonial concepts and practices."

This may indeed be part of "current Israeli discourse," but it is sadly not at all a part of the discourse among Jewish Americans, especially not among many over the age of about 40. I would argue that the vast chasm that has opened between many younger and older American Jews and their organizations (according to a myriad of polls) is in no small part due to a failure to confront the reality of what was done in 1947-49.

One of Zochrot's key publications is: *Erased from Space and Consciousness: Israel and the Depopulated Palestinian Villages of 1948* by Noga Kadman, published in 2015 by Zochrot and available in Hebrew, Arabic and English. Quoting from its description:

> "Hundreds of Palestinian villages were left empty across Israel when their residents became refugees after the 1948 war, their lands and property confiscated. Most of the villages were razed by the new State of Israel and in dozens, communities of Jews were settled—many refugees in their own right. The state embarked upon a systematic effort of renaming and remaking the landscape, and the Arab presence was all but erased from official maps and histories. Israelis are familiar with the ruins, terraces, and orchards that mark these sites today—almost half located within tourist areas or national parks; but they rarely receive any official information about the Arab communities that existed there, and about how they came to be depopulated and ruined. Using official archives, kibbutz publications, and visits to the former village

sites, Noga Kadman has reconstructed this history of erasure, which supplemented the physical destruction of the villages."

Another source is *Once Upon a Land/Omrim Yeshna Eretz – A Tour Guide,* by Tomer Gardi et al, published in 2012 in Hebrew and Arabic by Zochrot and Pardes Publications. This guide describes "18 tours in Palestinian neighborhoods and villages whose inhabitants **were expelled** by Israel during the Nakba and largely destroyed." (emphasis added) This book was reviewed in *Haaretz* (Dec. 7, 2012) in an article by Moshe Gilad under the title: *"The Arab villages that were: A new Israeli guidebook: A new volume in Hebrew and Arabic retraces a past that many prefer to forget."* In this review article, Gilad says:

> "Regarding the book, let me say straightaway that its importance goes beyond the mere fact of its publication. It contains consistent, systematic historical documentation, with a clear political opinion, of a past we tend to ignore....I'd visited these places before, but this time went in search of their Palestinian past – to see what remains of that past, which to me had been almost entirely transparent for decades. I looked for what could be found today of the villages... The guide presents the reader with complex challenges, such as dealing with a combination of tour directions and comprehensive history – and all in two languages."

The Nakba Map: Localities in the country that were destroyed between the beginning of Zionist colonization and the 1967 war, by Eitan Bronstein Aparicio, et al, published in March 2015 by Zochrot and Pardes Publications. This is the 2nd edition and is an updated version of the previous Nakba Map published in 2013. This map is in two layers. The first layer shows the locations of 601 Palestinian villages and urban neighborhoods and their populations before they were destroyed or emptied, and also the locations of 22 Israeli settlements that were destroyed in 1948, most of which were retaken within weeks. The map also shows the location of 194 Syrian villages destroyed or emptied in the 1967 conflict. The Palestinian locations range from Jaffa (76,000), Haifa (70,000), and Ramle (17,890) (33 areas of over 3000 inhabitants) to small settlements of less than 50 people. It includes only a few of the destroyed Bedouin villages due to difficulties in determining exact locations. The 601 Palestinian areas include 57 villages taken over by Jewish settlers prior to 1947. The second layer of the map provides an overlay that shows the names of the Israeli cities and towns that exist today, most of which sit on top of prior Palestinian sites.

The publication of this map was reviewed in *Haaretz* (July 31, 2015) by Amira Hass under the title *"Destruction of Palestinian villages is not a matter of perspective: An NGO has issued a second edition of its successful Nakba map, showing 601 Palestinian villages and 194 Syrian villages destroyed in 1947 and 1967, respectively, as well as destroyed Jewish communities."* The title is quoted in full to demonstrate that any reader of the newspaper would immediately know what this map was about. In the article Haas writes:

> "Most Israelis are not familiar with the map, which hangs in nearly every Palestinian home and bears the dense dots that represent the numerous Palestinian villages that existed before 1948...The mappers review (for the 2nd edition) led to an increase – from 14 to 20 – in the number of Palestinian communities still in existence where a section of residents were permanently or temporarily **expelled** in 1948. These are not part of the 601 destroyed villages...The new research ...revealed that Israel destroyed 194 Syrian villages and farms in 1967, containing 82,709 residents...and destroyed six Palestinian villages following the Six-Day War (1967)." (emphasis added)

Haas goes on to quote Bronstein Aparicio as saying:

> "The destruction and logic of the destruction is one of the foundations of the Israeli regime. Without understanding the pattern, it's impossible to understand what Israel is doing **today**..." (emphasis added)

Finally, on May 2, 2014, Ian Black in The Guardian (U.K.) wrote an article: *"Remembering the Nakba: Israel group puts 1948 Palestine back on the map: Zochrot aims to educate Israeli Jews – through tours and a new phone app – about a history obscured by enmity and denial,"* This GPS based app was updated in April 2015 and is available in Hebrew, Arabic and English. It provides location information, names of prior Palestinian villages, prior population figures, and brief histories.

28

The point of listing all of these materials by Zochrot, and the reviews in the Israeli and British press, is to demonstrate that evidence of this history is widely and publicly available, especially in Israel. Many, perhaps even most, Israelis know what happened, even if they choose to ignore or deny it. Every bit as important, almost all Palestinians have been keenly aware of this history since 1948, and in recent years have had their memory of those events validated and reinforced by the work of Jewish Israeli New Historians in academic books and in the popular press, and by the work by Israeli NGOs such as Zochrot. Ironically, it seems that Jewish Americans are far less aware, or accepting, of this history than Jewish Israelis. This ignorance or denial plays a major role in the way Jewish Israelis and Americans alike perceive the legitimacy of the grievances of Palestinians and how they think about the sort of remedies they are willing to consider in the face of Palestinian demands.

Palestinian Reaction to the Failure of Jewish Israelis and Americans to Acknowledge this History
In light of this history and the available knowledge of it, is it any wonder that the decedents of those Palestinians demand that they at least receive an apology and compensation from Israel for what was done to their parents and grandparents? From my own interactions, I can attest to the fact that Palestinians often argue:

> Were not the Germans forced to pay compensation to the survivors of the Holocaust? Is it not the case that the Israeli and American Jewish communities are quick to condemn with great moral righteousness the failure of Austria or Poland or Italy to admit their complicity in the Holocaust? They note the outrage of Jews about the failure of the French, until very recently, to acknowledge that country's role in the Holocaust. Did even the Americans not eventually apologize and make at least token payments to Japanese American families who lost their homes and businesses and were forced into camps during World War II? They note how often Japan is challenged even today to acknowledge and apologize for what they did to the Koreans and Chinese in World War II. Rather than hearing condemnations of the atrocities that the Americans committed against their own native population, they hear all too many members of the American and Israeli Jewish communities point to what was done in the U.S. and make comments that one should stop complaining about what the Israelis did and do to the Palestinians – after all, look what Americans did and do to their indigenous peoples.

Hence, Palestinians go on to ask: Why should we not be entitled to at least an apology and something more than just token compensation? Instead, all too many Jewish Israelis and Americans either still deny this history of ethnic cleansing and massacres and the destruction or occupation of Palestinian villages, or they express opinions such as:

> Well it may have happened. But that was almost a century ago. We, today, are not responsible. Why should we apologize? Why should we pay any compensation? Clearly we are never going to let "them" all back into Israel; after all, as you've shown, most of their old villages and neighborhoods don't even exist anymore. Where would they go? And besides, if we let them back into Israel they would be a majority and we would either lose the essence of being a "Jewish State" (more on that topic later) or we would lose our democracy. So no acknowledgement, no apology, no compensation, and by the way they must acknowledge Israel as a 'Jewish State.'

But until and unless Jewish Israelis at least acknowledge this history and demonstrate some degree of remorse and responsibility for it, peace is highly unlikely to occur.

Conclusions Regarding the Wars of 1947-48 and the Myths about them
So what is one to conclude from this discussion of the Wars of 1947-49? The conclusion should be clear -- the five myths are just that – myths – they are **not true.** This is not a contention or interpretation or opinion. This conclusion is factual, it is based upon hard and available historical evidence. At least since the Israeli fifty-year freedom of information act led in the late 1990s to the opening of the archives from 1947-49, it is clear that:

- The Jewish settlers in Palestine did **not** accept the recommendations of the U.N. Partition Plan boundaries, but choose to expand their territory far beyond even the 55.5% of the land of Palestine identified in that plan.

- The war did **not** begin in May 1948 when Israel declared its independence and the five Arab armies invaded. It began five months earlier, within hours of the vote in the U.N. General Assembly, and both sides had been preparing for this war long before that. Moreover, by May 1948, Israel had already conquered and occupied more than the specified 55.5% of the land.
- The Jewish settlers/Israelis were **never militarily outnumbered** as compared to the Palestinians and the Arab Liberation Army in 1947-48, or even as compared to the five Arab armies after the invasions of May 1948. In fact, they enjoyed superiority in the number of fighters of often more than 2 to 1, sometimes 3 to 1, during most of both wars. In terms of armaments, the Israelis while initially lacking heavy arms, rather quickly gained near parity in that regard, even succeeding in securing air superiority within a few months and bombed inside Egypt. Moreover, the officers in the Settler/Israeli forces were far better trained and were able to exercise a degree of coordinated command and control far superior to that of either the Palestinians or the invading Arab armies.
- The Jewish settlers/Israelis indeed did pursue a planned and well-executed program of **ethnic cleansing** to drive the Palestinians out of the land they intended to control, despite public comments to the contrary at the time, and since then.
- The Israelis did commit not one, but **numerous massacres** of unarmed men, women and children and this was widely known and discussed among the Palestinian population at the time. The fear of this did supplement and support the ethnic cleansing campaign in motivating the exodus of Palestinians. In comparison, there were "only" three incidents of massacres of Israelis.

Why must we debunk Israel's founding myths?

But one might well ask – so what? This all happened almost 70 years ago. Why raise it now? Are you not just looking for an excuse to verbally attack Israel, weaken it and undermine its legitimacy? After which, if the person raising these issues happens to be Jewish, the next statement is typically -- so why are you a self-hating Jew, and really an anti-Semite? (See the last section of this paper for a discussion of the role of charges of anti-Semitism.)

The truth is exactly the opposite. I am convinced that if Israel does not move quickly to recognize and help establish the State of Palestine alongside the State of Israel, the damage to Israel will be severe in terms of its own economy, its security, its total isolation among the nations of the world and even its growing alienation from the world's Jewish community and from its only ally, the U.S. And I am convinced that the failure to confront the falseness of these myths is a significant element in preventing Israel from reaching such an agreement to create two states, side-by-side, with security for both.

Recall the earlier discussion about the Israeli/Jewish sense of victimhood. These foundational myths discussed in the two sections about the creation of Israel serve a purpose. That is why they are defended so strongly, even though they are not true. (Recall the admonitions by Krugman and Orwell at the beginning of this paper.) These myths support the image that Israel is a moral, virtuous State created in a near empty landscape (except for a small minority of Jews who had lived there for centuries), indeed that it is a state honorably created by the U.N. after the horrors of the Holocaust. How often does one hear such statements as: How dare anyone worry about the Palestinians? What moral claim do they have to this land? Let them return to their real home in Jordan. At the same time, Israel clings to the image of itself as the small, weak David constantly confronted by the big, stronger Goliath. As we have discussed, Israelis are conditioned by centuries of history as victims to now live in fear: in fear of the Palestinians, in Gaza if not in the West Bank, in fear of the surrounding Arab States, in fear of Iran, in fear of Muslims generally, in fear of the U.N. and the many nations there that keep questioning Israel's commitment to human rights, in fear of being abandoned by the U.S., etc., etc., etc.

It is essential that Israel and the Israeli public find the courage to begin to see themselves in a more realistic light. While their fear in 1947-49 was **not** unreasonable at the time; in retrospect they must admit that they were far and away the stronger military force. They did not win that war against five Arab states, other volunteers from abroad, and the Palestinians by accident. In fact, they were not the David, they were the Goliath. Their victory was not a fluke, or good luck, or divine intervention. Without getting into details, it was also not an accident that they would have won in 1956 (if the U.S. had not forced Israel, Britain and France to back off from the attack on Egypt), that they did win in 1967 and in just 6 days, and won again in 1973. It is the case that they have the strongest and best trained military anywhere in the Middle East. They have the deterrence power that comes with being the only regional nation with nuclear weapons and with the means to deliver them by land, air and sea. They are also the only one with a sophisticated missile defense system. So why is Israel always acting so fearful and defensive?

The Iran Nuclear Agreement Issue (Formally called the Joint Comprehensive Plan of Action (JCPOA))
As this was being written, there was a new example of how the Israeli government, especially under Netanyahu, practices and uses, perhaps cynically, the politics of fear. In August 2015, the P5+1 negotiations with Iran concluded and the various nations then began to go through what might be called their ratification and implementation procedures. P5+1 refers to the five permanent members of the U.N. Security Council: the U.S., Britain, France, Russian and China, and the +1 refers to Germany. The negotiations also included a representative of the E.U. So including Iran, there were really 8 parties around the table. (In the document itself it refers to this group as the E3/EU+3.) This agreement (it is not formally a treaty) is the culmination of a 2-year negotiation process to prevent Iran from acquiring nuclear weapons in exchange for the lifting of economic and political sanctions that were imposed on Iran to bring them to the table on this issue.

Let us address the worst-case scenario first. While it is obvious that there is a strong international consensus that Iran should be kept from acquiring nuclear weapons, the question still must be asked specifically: Why was\is Israel so afraid of Iran acquiring a nuclear weapon? Iran is hardly suicidal. [See for example, Peter Beinart: *Iran's Leaders Are Not Suicidal*, (The Atlantic, March 2, 2015) or his article *Iran is not an 'existential' threat to Israel – no matter what Netanyahu claims (Haaretz,* August 7, 2015)]. Iran's leaders know that their nation would cease to exist if it attacked Israel given that Israel has the capacity to deliver multiple nuclear weapons by land, air and sea. Mutual deterrence, in part based upon second strike capability, worked between the USSR and the West for decades. Most observers agree that it would work between Israel and Iran. So while no one wants Iran to acquire a nuclear weapons capacity; at the same time, it is not really the existential threat that Netanyahu keeps claiming it is.

It is also certainly true that there are other strategic issues involved, beyond the safety of Israel, that motivate the international community to want to prevent Iran from acquiring nuclear weapons. These include avoiding a nuclear arms race in the Middle East, not increasing tensions between Iran and the Sunni Arab nations, avoiding the possibilities of Iran becoming a nuclear regional and even world power, etc. But those are not the motivating issues that were used in Israel, and with the more conservative elements of the American Jewish community, to oppose the Iran nuclear agreement. Instead, it was, yet again, fear, not global strategy, which was the Israeli government's focus. And in all the fearmongering what was lost was the fact that the agreement, while not perfect, is the only alternative available which would block Iran from acquiring a nuclear weapon for at least 10 to 15 years. In fact, some elements are binding for 25 years and others are binding permanently. Whereas, without the implementation of this agreement, it is widely estimated that Iran's "breakout time" to acquire such a weapon would be only a matter of months. (To read the full text of the agreement, go to:
http://apps.washingtonpost.com/g/documents/world/full-text-of-the-iran-nuclear-deal/1651/)

In fact, according to widespread published reports, Israel's military intelligence corps, in defiance of orders from Netanyahu, wrote a report on the Iran agreement and leaked it to the press. The report was quite balanced and concluded that the agreement reduces the likelihood of Iran attacking Israel and "provides a 10 year window during which Iran will not be able to develop nuclear weapons," but during which Israel will be "free to develop new countermeasures." The report indicated that the upsides of the agreement "while not perfect, are real" and that the downsides are "manageable and not too calamitous" for them [the Israeli military and national security forces] to cope with. This report was consistent with public statements by many retired Israeli military and national security personnel who stated that the Iran agreement was acceptable and the best alternative available.

In fact, many of these security experts argued that the tone and nature of Netanyahu's opposition to the agreement was causing major damage to Israel's national security.

> (See the newspaper article: *Netanyahu Must Stop Silencing Intel Chiefs Who Find Deal Acceptable: There are those in the Intelligence Corps whose views on the nuclear agreement are at odds with Netanyahu's position; their opinions are being kept from the public,* Amir Oren, Haaretz, Aug 10, 2015. See also *The Game-Changing Iran Report that Bibi Fears*, J.J. Goldberg. The Forward, Aug. 21, 2015

The question Goldberg and others are asking is: Why then was Netanyahu causing so much damage to Israel's interests by opposing this agreement in the manner he was doing?

It is sad, but likely true, that key rightwing politicians in Israel knew that they can play on the Jewish feelings of victimhood and fear, and knew they could use the Iran issue to distract the Israeli public from the far more serious issue of the need to forge a viable Two-State agreement. In fact, they have been systematically doing this for years, long before this agreement was reached. This distraction is also a useful foil to keep attention away from a range of very pressing domestic Israeli issues. So while some opponents of this agreement may be quite sincere, though misinformed, others who choose to ignore Israel's own security establishment cynically used this issue for their own political purposes – and one has to put Netanyahu at the head of the list of those almost surely in this camp.

Moreover, what is lost in Netanyahu's fearmongering was the fact that there were no alternatives to this agreement, another point recognized by Israel's own intelligence corps. In particular, Israel's own military and national security leaders understood that a military attack on Iran was not feasible and would make matters worse – which is why they blocked three (some claim four) earlier efforts by Netanyahu to mount such an attack, according to Ehud Barak, former Prime Minister, Defense Minister and military Chief of Staff.

> This was widely reported, for example see: *Barak: Netanyahu wanted to strike Iran in 2010 and 2011, but colleagues blocked him.* The Times of Israel, Aug. 21, 2015; also *Israel Army Blocked Netanyahu's Plan to Attack Iran: Former Defense Minister Ehud Barak*, Global Research Newsletter, Aug, 24, 2015. For a particularly insightful analysis of what happened see *The Morten Three* (referring to the three Israeli officials who blocked Netanyahu) by Uri Avnery, Aug 29, 2015, http://zope.gush-shalom.org/home/en/channels/avnery

The suggestion by Netanyahu and others that a better deal could be negotiated was patently absurd, given that none of the negotiating participants (Britain, France, Germany, China, Russia, the E.U. and Iran) would support such an effort. There was even a meeting of representatives from France, Germany and Britain with members of the U.S. Congress where this point was made explicit. Quite to the contrary, it was been made clear that if the U.S. Congress were to refuse to lift their sanctions, the rest of the world, including the U.N., would render that effort close to useless by lifting all the sanctions over which they had control and by moving quickly to establish full trade relations with Iran. And this U.S. Administration was and is highly unlikely to veto the Security Council's efforts to go forward with the agreement. Indeed, the 15 members of the U.N. Security Council already voted unanimously (a rare event) to endorse the Iran Agreement. So no matter what Israel said or wanted, and even if Israel and elements of the Jewish American community, working with the Republican party, were to have succeeded in manipulating events in the U.S. Congress to block the U.S.'s full implementation of the agreement, all that this blocking effort would have achieved would have been to further isolate Israel from the world community, make a mockery of U.S. diplomatic efforts, and focus international anger on both Israel and the U.S. Fortunately, it is clear as of this writing, that the efforts by the Israeli government, supported in the U.S. by the American Israel Political Affairs Committee (AIPAC) and the Republican Party, failed to block the U.S.'s participation in implementing the agreement.

There was/is another element of Israeli/Jewish concern about the Iran nuclear agreement that needs to be addressed. Moreover, it needs to be noted that this is a concern that others in the region, especially Sunni Arab nations, share. This is the fact that Iran will reap a financial windfall, first from the release of its frozen funds now held in foreign banks and second from the revenue from its oil which it will be allowed to sell again, as the agreement is implemented. There is talk of a $150 billion windfall. Might Iran use some of that money to try to strengthen Hezbollah and Hamas as Netanyahu and AIPAC asserted? There will be many other claims on the money, both internally in Iran and in other foreign endeavors, especially in Iraq, Syria and Yemen (all of which worry the Sunni powers). In fact, Sunni Hamas is negotiating with Saudi Arabia in an effort to offset any loss of support from Shia Iran due to the support Hamas gave to those rebelling against Assad in Syria. Hamas is even negotiating with Israel according to many reports (see the article: *Is there a long-term Israel-Hamas agreement in the works*, Zvi Bar'el, Haaretz, Aug 17, 2015). Shia Hezbollah's forces are over-extended fighting in Syria – starting a conflict with Israel is very low on its priorities. But despite all this, might some of the money find its way either directly, or in military goods purchased/produced, to Hezbollah or Hamas? Sure. But the best way to provoke an attack on Israel by these groups, or by Iran itself, is to encourage a military attack on Iran in lieu of this negotiated agreement. Moreover, as cited earlier, Israel's military intelligence establishment considers this new flow of money a risk that while not desirable, is quite manageable.

The hard fact was that Israel was the only nation to officially oppose this agreement. Moreover it did so in a manner that isolated Israel from the rest of the world, that weakened Israel's relation to the U.S., and that forced major splits within the American Jewish community and between major elements of the American Jewish and Israeli Jewish communities. To pay this price based upon exaggerated fears of increased support for Hamas and Hezbollah is yet another example of Israel playing upon the politics of fear, not of rational policy determination. Israel, under Netanyahu, once again fell victim to its own worst fears, and did so in a manner that rational analysis would argue hurt its own best interests. Is it not time to examine and confront the roots of these fears, of this sense of victimhood, and move on to rational self-interest? And this concern assumes the best of Netanyahu; that is, that his fears are/were real and honest. If instead he was "merely" cynically using these fears to manipulate public and political opinion both in Israel and among many Jewish Americans, then we must ask why does this tactic work, why are Jewish Israelis and Americans so willing to allow themselves to be manipulated by their fears? Revealing the falsity of the myths underlying these fears is the core purpose of this paper.

The Emigration of Arab Jews from the Middle East and North Africa
We at least need to touch upon a separate issue that is often raised when evaluating the *Nakba*, the catastrophic (for the Palestinians) departure of more than 700,000 Palestinians from their homes, villages and farms in the 1947-49 period.   There are many supporters of Israel who point to the fact that out of the one million or so Mizrahi and Sephardic Jews who lived in other Middle Eastern and North African nations (including Turkey and Iran) in the early 1940s, all but a few thousand emigrated to Israel starting in 1944 and continuing thereafter. Many Israeli and American Jews point out that many, perhaps most, of these Arab Jews were driven out of their home by the hostile actions of those Middle Eastern and North African governments. Ultimately, about 700,000 went to Israel, about 126,000 between 1948 and 1951, 90% from Iraq, Libya and Yemen. (Those in Iran did not emigrate until the 1980s.)

However, two caveats need to be acknowledged. First, Zionist organizations developed what they called the "One Million Plan" in 1944 to attract and encourage this immigration into Palestine/Israel as a way to boost the Jewish population, and this effort intensified during the 1947-49 period and immediately thereafter. Second, many of these Arab Jews voluntarily moved to Israel after 1949, attracted by the possibility of living in a predominately Jewish nation. There is an intense debate among historians about the push / pull factors behind this immigration – how many were pushed out by "their" governments and how many were pulled toward Israel by its offers of subsidized travel and housing. I do not wish to get into that discussion here. Instead I want to make a different point. All too many Israeli and American Jews try to conflate the emigration, forced or voluntary, of Palestinians out of Israel with the immigration of these Arab Jews – as if one balanced the other. One often hears statements like – "Well these Arab and North African nations drove out "their" Jews, why should one condemn Israel for driving out "its" Palestinians?" But as the old adage goes, one bad deed does not excuse another. Even to the extent that Jews indeed were driven out of many Arab and North African states, that provides not one iota of moral or political justification for the ethnic cleansing, massacres and forced deportation of the Palestinians in

1947-49 or for the destruction of Palestinian housing and the seizing of Palestinian land today. These expulsions of Jews were hardly the fault of the Palestinians, any more than they had responsibility for the Holocaust. On the contrary, pointing to the expulsion of the Arab Jews is simply a cynical effort to avoid accepting responsibility for what Israel did and does to the Palestinians.

Summary - Why Israel Needs to Acknowledge Its History

Israel has to examine and own up to its history not in order to weaken itself, but to find the strength to see itself as the Goliath that is quite capable of:

a) taking the risk to confront the racism so inherent in the attitudes toward Palestinians
b) acknowledging how and why most of the Palestinians became refugees. And while not necessarily allowing for more than a token number to return, at least finding the strength and compassion to apologize and offer some compensation
c) finding the strength to take the risk of finally negotiating a Two-State Solution, not out of concern for the Palestinians (though this would be admirable), but in Israel's own best interests
d) supporting the agreement by six leading nations of the international community with Iran to block the latter's development of nuclear weapons.

The question is whether Israeli and American Jews can find the courage and intellectual integrity to confront Israel's historical behavior during the 1947-49 wars, including the ethnic cleansing and the massacres of Palestinian civilians. More recently, can they confront Israel's behavior during its multiple wars on Gaza, including the totally disproportionate killing and wounding of Palestinian women, children and the elderly in Gaza, as the soldiers of the organization Breaking the Silence have, instead of condemning these courageous Israeli men and women? Can they find the strength and integrity to confront Israel's history of harassment and persecution of Palestinians, its pattern of midnight break-ins into Palestinian homes and the pulling of people out of bed, the shooting at peaceful demonstrators including children, the administrative detentions without charges or trials of hundreds of Palestinians, including children as young as 7, the housing demolitions and collective punishments for the acts of individuals, the refusal to allow Palestinians to build homes in their own areas while supporting the illegal (according to the Israeli Supreme Court) theft of Palestinian land to build settlements upon? Can they face the fact that the behavior of this State has come to resemble that of governments who victimized Jews over the centuries? Can they let go of their sense of victimhood, their consuming fears, find their strength, admit their errors, and build a better society for both themselves and for the Palestinians (both for those who are Israeli citizens and those who wish to build their own state)? This is why it is necessary to reexamine these founding myths – not to weaken Israel, but to strengthen it.

Part III - Four Current Myths about the Prospects for a Two-State Solution

There remain four other myths that must be addressed if we are to see movement toward a Two-State Solution

Myth #12: Palestine Cannot Exist as a Nation State until and unless Israel Recognizes It as Such

The only way for Israel and Israelis to re-claim the moral legitimacy that they say they value so highly is to return to the principles embedded in the original partition plan and endorse the creation of a State of Palestine alongside the State of Israel. In this regard it should be noted that, on November 15, 1988, the Palestine Liberation Organization published the Palestinian Declaration of Independence citing Resolution 181, arguing that the resolution continues to provide international legitimacy for the right of the Palestinian people to sovereignty and national independence. Many scholars have written in support of this view. A General Assembly request in 1988 to the International Court of Justice (ICJ) for an advisory opinion on this matter specifically cited resolution 181 as a "relevant resolution." In response to the request for an advisory opinion, Judge Abdul Koroma in explaining the resulting majority opinion said:

"The Court has also held that the right of self-determination as an established and recognized right under international law applies to the territory and to the Palestinian people. Accordingly, the exercise of such right entitles the Palestinian people to a State of their own as originally envisaged in resolution 181."

Note that the ICJ based its ruling on the right of self-determination, and only referred to 181 as an historical vision. It should be noted further that as of October 30, 2014, 135 (69.9%) of the 193 member states of the United Nations had recognized the State of Palestine. In four other European nations, including France and Britain, their parliaments have recommended to their governments that they recognize the State of Palestine. To this list one must add the Vatican, which recognized Palestine as a state in May 2015. Many of the countries that do not recognize the State of Palestine nevertheless recognize the PLO as the "representative of the Palestinian people". On November 29, 2012, the U.N. General Assembly passed a motion changing Palestine's "entity" status to "non-member observer state" by a vote of 138 to 9, with 41 abstentions, a more overwhelmingly affirmative vote than the one supporting the Partition plan in 1947. In September, 2015, the U.N. General Assembly decided (by 119 yes-8 no-45 abstentions) that both Palestine and the Vatican (which have the same status of "non-member observer state"), are allowed to fly their flags at the U.N. alongside those of the member states. **One could with some legitimacy claim that the State of Palestine exists today, even if Israel and the U.S. refuse to recognize it.**

In fact, Israel has vigorously complained every time the Palestinians reached out to the U.N to try to establish their legitimate right to statehood. Instead, Israel acts exactly like the European colonial nations who demanded that it was up to them and them alone to decide when to grant independence to their former colonies. The fact is that as a matter of international law, the Palestinians have the same right to simply declare their independence and establish their State as the Israelis and the Americans did – and indeed they have done so. If Israel then decides to attack the newly declared State of Palestine, just as the French, British and Portuguese did when their colonies declared independence, or to attempt to strangle it economically, they can do that and bear whatever consequences the members of the international community seek to impose. Instead, Israel and much of the world's Jewish community has acted shocked and dismayed by the fact that many nations in Europe and elsewhere have begun to apply economic pressure upon Israel to recognize the State of Palestine.

It certainly needs to be acknowledged that even if the State of Palestine were recognized as legitimate and existing, this would not settle many outstanding issues – perhaps most importantly the exact boundaries of that state. Clearly that would require negotiations between Israel and Palestine as to where the border between them would be drawn and what exchanges of land might be enacted as part of that process. Similarly, if the State of Palestine embraces both the West Bank and the Gaza strip and if Palestine wished to have those two places connected, there would have to be negotiations between the two states as to how that might occur; e.g. via rail through Israel. But these would be negotiations between two sovereign states, not between a State and an illegally occupied, and many would claim colonialized, territory. The illegality of moving of Israeli citizens into "the Occupied Palestinian Territory" (the official U.N. designation), has been asserted by **every** nation on earth except Israel. But some things *technically* would not need to be negotiated, such as Palestine's right to build an international airport or to build a sea port in Gaza. However, Israel could, and almost surely would, continue to make such infrastructure projects impossible by the blockade it has imposed on Gaza and the limitations it imposes on imports into the West Bank from abroad. But one could argue that such actions on the part of Israel against another sovereign state, Palestine, under international law would be illegal and, indeed, could be interpreted as acts of war. Whether such legal interpretations would give Israel any pause is doubtful, since they have chosen, with virtual impunity, to ignore many aspects of international law.

But so long as Israel and the U.S. refuse to acknowledge the existence of a Palestinian state and so long as Israel maintains its power to occupy and colonize the West Bank, patrol it with its army, subject its people to a military not civil justice system, decide who can build where, and enforces an armed blockade of Gaza, the existence of a Palestinian state is a moot issue. At the same time, it is necessary for Fatah and Hamas to build a functioning unity government for the State of Palestine to be viable. Admittedly, this is made almost impossible by the efforts of the U.S. and Israel to block the formation of such a government and by their refusal to negotiate with it – even when such a government consists of competent people not representing either Fatah or Hamas, but acknowledged by both. By the same token, for a viable State of Palestine to claim to exist, the legal and security systems in Gaza and the West Bank must be merged and brought under the control of a central unity government. So despite the fact that to a large extent the State of Palestine already exists, we must address the issue of the likelihood of success of negotiations between Israel and the Palestinians, whether the latter are viewed as citizens of a State or as residents of a territory under occupation.

Myth #13: The Issues that must be resolved to reach an agreement that would ensure the recognition of Two States, Israel and Palestine, living side-by-side with security for both, are so complex and the disagreements about these issues are so severe, that achieving such an agreement is almost impossible. Moreover, the existence of the Jewish settlements in the West Bank and East Jerusalem renders such an agreement infeasible.

This is a near fatal myth, since if one believes that the complexities are so overwhelming, then there is little point in trying to maintain the hope for a Two-State Solution, never mind trying to foster negotiations to that end in the near term. Similarly, if one believes that the existence of the settlements has created a situation that renders any attempt to find a mutually acceptable border virtually impossible, then there is little point in trying to get negotiations started. But both parts of this myth are **not** true. In fact, one could well argue that those fostering this myth are doing so cynically, because it serves their purpose of blocking movement toward the creation of two states.

What are the **key issues** to be resolved?
1. **Borders** and the Future of the **Settlements** and the **Settlers** (not the same)
   a. Western Border between Israel and the West Bank
   b. Eastern Border in the Jordan River Valley with Jordan
   c. Southern Border regarding Gaza and Egypt, Gaza and Israel
   d. The borders in the Golan Heights with Syria and in the north with Lebanon are not issues for discussion with the Palestinians
   e. Settlers: If on Israeli side of new border, then they simply remain Israeli citizens. But if they are on the Palestinian side, do they stay or not and if they stay, with what status?
2. **Security** for Israel and for Palestine along borders a, b, c above and from/within West Banks and Gaza
   a. Who is to have what forces where, armed with what, and how guaranteed?
3. **Jerusalem** –
   a. How to define its borders? Who controls what? Who can go where?
   b. Do Jewish settlers in East Jerusalem stay or go and if they stay, what is their status?
   c. How does the status of Palestinians in East Jerusalem change? (Now have Israeli resident permits.)
4. **Water Rights** – How administered and how allocated, possibly regionally
5. **Right of Return of Palestinians**
   a. from where, to where and who is a refugee?
   b. is there to be an apology?
   c. is there to be compensation in lieu of return and, if so, how much and to whom?
6. **Palestine as a Contiguous State** – How to connect Gaza and the West Bank?
7. **Palestinian Access to the Outside World** – by land, air, and sea
8. A New Issue: **Recognition of Israel as a "*Jewish State*"** – not "merely" as
      "The National Home for Jews"

In a series of previous papers and public lectures, I have discussed all of the first seven items in some detail, as have many others, and it is not the purpose of this paper to rehash that. Obviously there have been many negotiating efforts to address most or all of these issues. The point to be made here is that, while none of those efforts were ultimately successful, what is not widely understood is the extent to which the terms for settling **all** of the first seven issues are already well known by both sides. While the Bill Clinton sponsored Camp David talks in

2000 failed, largely over the map of borders he proposed, which the Palestinians found unacceptable, there was agreement on virtually all of the other issues. What is not widely discussed is that those talks resumed (without the U.S.'s direct participation) the following year, 2001, at Taba, Israel.

The Taba Negotiations in 2001 – A Near Success

The talks at Taba succeeded in dealing with **all** of the first seven topics. (The "Jewish State" issue had not been raised by Israel at that time.) It is revealing and tragic to read the reports on why these **successful talks** were abandoned after both sides had agreed to the terms of settlement and they were in the final stages of perfecting the exact wording of the agreement. The breakdown is attributed to the political circumstances posed by the pending Israeli elections and the changeover in leadership in the United States from Clinton to Bush. The negotiators had run out of political time. They could not conclude an agreement with Clinton now out of office and Barak (the Israeli Prime Minister) standing for reelection in two weeks. **"We made progress, substantial progress. We are closer than ever to the possibility of striking a final deal,"** said Shlomo Ben-Ami, Israel's head negotiator. Saeb Erekat, Palestinian chief negotiator, said, **"My heart aches because I know we were so close. We need six more weeks to conclude the drafting of the agreement."** The point is that it was clear after Taba that the terms of a possible settlement were well understood by all parties, and that the situation was not so complex that no solution was feasible. The issue was not and is not complexity, but political will.

Two weeks later, Ariel Sharon of the conservative Likud party was elected replacing Barak and the Labor party government. This new Israeli government immediately sent a letter to the newly elected President Bush and to the Palestinians stating that Israel would not be bound by any of the terms tentatively agreed to at Taba. Sharon then refused to enter into any new negotiations. Instead, Sharon accelerated the building of settlements and talked publicly of this effort as being like making a pastrami sandwich with slices of meat so closely packed together that it would be impossible for anyone to later pull them apart. This is a strange metaphor, but the statement was indicative of his intention to use the building of settlements to make it impossible to create a separate Palestinian state.

The Issue of the Term "The Jewish State" and the Legacy of Theodor Herzl

A new issue was raised for the first time by the prior (to the current one) Netanyahu government. (See # 8 in the above list of key issues to be resolved). This is the Israeli demand that the Palestinians expressly recognize Israel as a "Jewish State" as a precondition for beginning a new round of negotiations toward a Two-State solution. Looking at the numbers in Appendix B – "Population of Israel and Palestine in 2014," it is clear that 20.7% of Israeli citizens are ethnically Palestinian, and almost all of these are either Muslim (including some Druze) or Christian. Israel is going to have to decide if they are going to require these non-Jews to live as second class citizens in a theocratic state, or as full citizens in a democratic state. This is also tied to the fact that, as the figures at the bottom of Appendix B show, the total population in 2014 within Mandate Palestine (i.e. – in Israel, the West Bank and Gaza) was 6.2 million Jews and 6.14 million Palestinians, with the Palestinians sure to be in the majority by 2020. So if Israel does not agree to a Two-State solution very soon, it will be the case that the Jewish population will be a minority within a de facto one-state area – meaning that the Jewish Israelis will have to choose between being a minority in one democratic state or practicing apartheid to continue to maintain control over the majority of the people. The choice is real and stark. So one can only hope that the Israeli government decides to move toward a Two-State Solution, gives up the stipulation of being recognized as a Jewish State, and instead accepts being recognized as a democratic state that is acknowledged as providing a homeland for any Jews who wish to live there. (See the Geneva Initiative accord summary in Appendix C for possible language.)

It is often noted that Theodor Herzl in 1896 published a book in German entitled *Der Judenstaat*, which in its English translation is entitled *The Jewish State*. Later (1902) he wrote a novel, *Altneuland*, which described life in this *Judenstaat*. The novel's title translates as The Old New Land. The relevant issue is how Herzl's vision of The Jewish State compares to the current vision of Netanyahu and Israeli conservatives. Are they, in fact, being true to Herlz's dream?

In *The Jewish State*, Herzl wrote:

> "Shall we end by having a theocracy? No, indeed. Faith unites us, knowledge gives us freedom. We shall therefore prevent any theocratic tendencies from coming to the fore on the part of our priesthood. We shall keep our priests within the confines of their temples … they must not interfere in the administration of the State… else they will conjure up difficulties without and within."

> "Every man will be as free and undisturbed in his faith or his disbelief as he is in his nationality. And if it should occur that men of other creeds and different nationalities come to live amongst us, we should accord them honorable protection and equality before the law."
> (From section V of *The Jewish State* - www.jewishvirtuallibrary.org/jsource/Zionism/herzl2.html)

In Old-New Land, Herzl elaborated on this vision:

> "Matters of faith were once and for all excluded from public influence. … Whether anyone sought religious devotion in the synagogue, in the church, in the mosque, in the art museum, or in a philharmonic concert, did not concern society. That was his private affair."

> "It [the Jewish state] is founded on the ideas which are a common product of all civilized nations. … It would be immoral if we would exclude anyone, whatever his origin, his descent, or his religion, from participating in our achievements. For we stand on the shoulders of other civilized peoples. … What we own we owe to the preparatory work of other peoples. Therefore, we have to repay our debt. There is only one way to do it, the highest tolerance. Our motto must therefore be, now and ever: 'Man, you are my brother'." (Quoted from Altneuland in *Zionism and the Jewish National Idea*, 1970, pg 189)

In his diary, Herzl wrote:

> "It goes without saying that we shall respectfully tolerate persons of other faiths and protect their property, their honor, and their freedom with the harshest means of coercion. This is another area in which we shall set the entire world a wonderful example … Should there be many such immovable owners in individual areas [who would not sell their property to us], we shall simply leave them there and develop our commerce in the direction of other areas which belong to us".
> *(The Complete Diaries of Theodor Herzl*, Thomas Yoseloff, Herzl Press, 1960, pg 88/90)

Herzl was also clear about the issue of how the Jewish people were to acquire ownership over the land. It was to be purchased. But he was very concerned that these purchases be sanctioned by some sovereign power, arguing that:

> "Important experiments in colonization have been made, though on the mistaken principle of a gradual infiltration of Jews. An infiltration is bound to end badly. It continues till the inevitable moment when the native population feels itself threatened, and forces the government to stop a further influx of Jews. Immigration is consequently futile unless we have the sovereign right to continue such immigration."
> (*The Jewish State*, translated by Sylvie d'Avigdor, Nutt, London, 1896, reprinted by Dover, 1988, p. 95.)

Hence, he made extensive, but unsuccessful efforts to have the Ottoman Empire sanction the purchases of Palestinian land by Jews. After that effort failed, the Zionist movement was successful in having the Balfour Declaration issued, and in securing the instructions by the League of Nations for the British Palestine Mandate to implement that declaration (as discussed earlier). This did indeed provide some sovereign protective oversight for the Jewish colonialization of Palestine.

On the other hand, Herzl was very straightforward about what was to happen to the people displaced by the purchases. He sought a "gentle" process, but at the same time advocated what would today have to be termed 'gentle ethnic cleansing' (something of an oxymoron). In his diary, he wrote:

"When we occupy the land, we shall bring immediate benefits to the state that receives us. We must expropriate gently the private property on the estates assigned to us. We shall try to spirit the penniless population across the border by procuring employment for it in the transit countries, while denying it any employment in our country. The property owners will come over to our side. Both the process of expropriation and the removal of the poor must be carried out discretely and circumspectly"
The Complete Diaries of Theodor Herzl, Thomas Yoseloff, Herzl Press, 1960, pg 88/90

In 1947-49, and then again in 1967, Israel apparently did not feel any responsibility to be "gentle," or to take only land sold willingly to it. Even today, in seizing Palestinian land upon which to build settlements, there seems little concern for doing so "discretely and circumspectly." The Israel envisioned by Herzl clearly is not the current State of Israel. Citing Herzl's work, *The Jewish State,* as a means to rationalize the demand today that the Palestinians must recognize Israel as a "Jewish State," either as a precondition for negotiations toward a Two-State solution, or failing that to demand that such recognition must be the outcome of such negotiations, seems to be a recipe for guaranteeing that there will be not be two states. Since it is highly unlikely that any Palestinian representatives will agree to codifying second class citizenship for the Palestinian citizens of Israel who constitute more than 20% of that nation's population.

Are the Settlements a Barrier to a Two-State Agreement?
To turn to the second element of Myth #13, it should be appreciated that a new border between Israel and Palestine is still feasible despite all the settlements that have been built and expanded on the West Bank and despite the number of Israelis who have been moved into East Jerusalem. Most of the settlement expansion has been quite close to the 1967 Green Line border. It is still feasible to draw a new border that would render Palestine viable and would bring about 58% of the West Bank settlers into Israel, leaving *only* about 147,000 in West Bank Palestine. Such a border would move only about 3-5% of the 1967 West Bank land into Israel (and would be exchanged for an equal amount of Israeli land to be added to the southern West Bank and to Gaza). Those settlers left would constitute only about 1.8% of the Israeli population. Under the terms set forth in the most recent Geneva Initiative discussed just below (and see Appendix C), the Jewish settlers left beyond the new boundary would be given the option of either staying in place or moving, with financial help, into Israel. Since many of them, perhaps the majority, are living in the West Bank for economic, not ideological, reasons, it is likely that many would move. Those choosing to remain in Palestine would retain Israeli citizenship, but would live as expats under Palestinian law, just as many Israelis live in Berlin and New York under German or U.S. law. No one would be forced to move. Similarly in Jerusalem, the terms recommended by the Geneva Initiative would give Israelis living in East Jerusalem (outside Jewish neighborhoods that would become part of Israel) the same options, while the Palestinians living in East Jerusalem would lose their Israeli residence permits and gain Palestinian citizenship. There would be guaranteed freedom of movement for everyone throughout the Old City.

The biggest problem on the West Bank is in and around the Ariel settlement that reaches far into Palestine, where most of the 147,000 settlers likely to be left on the Palestinian side of the border live. The biggest problem in the area of East Jerusalem is known as the E-1 zone. Right now that zone is largely empty. But if it were to be developed as a built-up Jewish settlement, it would cut off East Jerusalem from the rest of Palestine and be a deal breaker. Every Western nation, especially the U.S., has cautioned Israel not to develop the E-1 zone. But with the new Israeli government, some of whose members advocate the development of E-1 for just that reason, it remains to be seen what happens. Still, for now at least, it is still feasible to draw a new border that would be acceptable to most knowledgeable people on both sides.

The Issue of Water
Water is a crucial issue that would have to be addressed in any final agreement. Right now, the Jewish settlements sit on top of what is estimated to be 80% of the aquifer on the West Bank. Various streams and small rivers flow across both Settlement and Palestinian areas which present problems not only of access to water, but of pollution. In addition, there are issues of access to the Jordan River which impact not only Israel and the West

Bank, but also Jordan. Palestinian and Israeli water experts meet regularly to discuss these issues, and plans for a regional water authority are constantly updated. Such a regional authority is almost sure to be part of any final agreement.

Myth #14: Israel has been willing to accept a Two-State agreement, but the Palestinians have not.
It is also important to note that after Taba, it was not the Palestinians who walked away from an agreement, but the Israelis. The effort to forge a final settlement continued in later years (Madrid, Annapolis, then with first Mitchell and then Kerry serving as mediators). One can argue that the barriers to reaching a settlement put up by the Israelis were often the deal breakers. On the other hand, one of the efforts that made a good deal of progress was under Israeli Prime Minister Ehud Olmert, who was convinced that a Two-State agreement was in Israel's best interest. But his personal legal problems (he ended up being convicted of accepting bribes), ended his career and these efforts. But it was not the Palestinians who broke off these talks.

What many do not appreciate is that there were not just what political scientists refer to as Track 1 level talks (that is, with both sides officially represented by high level officers), but also talks at the Track 2 and Track 1 ½ level. Track 2 refers to talks at which high level personnel represent each side, but not as official representatives of their governments. The Oslo Agreements began as Track 2 and only toward the end became Track 1. In **Geneva, in 2003**, there were Track 1 ½ level talks (official Palestinian representatives, high level, but unofficial Israeli representatives), and these talks **succeeded completely**. (See Appendix C – The Geneva Initiative 2003 – Summary Agreement). The agreement included detailed maps of all the border areas, including in and around Jerusalem. The terms of the agreement reached in Geneva, which has come to be known as the **Geneva Initiative**, were not only completed and published in 2003, but **have been updated on an annual basis since them**.

The Geneva Initiative continues today organizationally, the proposed agreement is updated regularly, and the organization conducts regular training sessions to brief both Israeli and Palestinian officials/politicians and others about the terms of a feasible agreement given current conditions. At least 38 members of the newly elected (March 2015) Israeli Parliament, the Knesset, have participated in these training sessions. An interesting series of events happened in August 2015. To reduce the influence of a political rival, Mahmoud Abbas, officially the President the State of Palestine, closed the offices of the Palestinian Peace Coalition NGO which is dedicated to the implementation of the Geneva Initiative. According to a report in *Haaretz* (Aug 20, 2015), this NGO promotes the initiative and the Two-State Solution by working in a variety of Palestinian sectors of society and holds regular meetings of Palestinians and Israelis to develop strategies for the implementation of the initiative. There was an immediate backlash from a number of European Union governments which fund this effort. The pressure worked, and three days later Abbas reversed himself and withdrew the closure order. A similar NGO on the Israeli side continued to function throughout this incident, though it is regularly under pressure from the current (Netanyahu) Israeli government, which is not supportive of its efforts. Nevertheless, the point is that as the Taba talks and the Geneva process demonstrate; there is an interest by key factions on both sides in forging a Two-State solution and the likely terms of such an agreement are updated regularly and are well known by both sides.

Myth #15: The composition and politics of the current (as of May 2015) Netanyahu government of Israel render it virtually impossible that negotiations toward a Two-State Solution can even be undertaken in the near term. At the same time, the divided leadership (Fatah/Hamas) of the Palestinian Authority and the refusal of Hamas to accept the "three commitments" renders meaningful negotiations from the Palestinian side equally impossible. The prospect for movement toward a Two-State solution is virtually non-existent in the near future and we will inevitably see either more military conflict and/or movement toward the solidification of a de facto one-state, non-democratic, apartheid system.

The actual situation is more uncertain than this statement implies. Nevertheless, this scenario is certainly quite possible. To thoroughly analyze all the elements embedded in this Myth would take a lengthy paper or book. But let us explore very briefly how and why the outcome described in Myth #15 might be avoided and how significant movement toward a Two-State solution might occur.

See Appendix D for a table of **the most recent (March 2015) Israeli election results**, with a list of the parties in and out of the coalition government, and their positions on the Two-State Solution. As Appendix D shows, there are 120 seats in the Israeli parliament, called the Knesset. Netanyahu's coalition has only 61, the bare minimum to form a government. Any time one or two individuals in the coalition parties choose to, they can precipitate a crisis and force new elections. In terms of politics, especially on the issue of the creation of a Palestinian state and the continued building of settlements, this is the most rightwing government in Israeli history. This certainly does not bode well for the expectation for any movement toward negotiations.

However, there is a strange anomaly. Kahlon's Kulanu party (again see Appendix D), a member of the coalition government with 10 seats, actually supports the Two-State Solution, though it is not its priority concern: domestic economic issues are. But if a proposed Two-State agreement were brought to a vote in the Knesset, most of the ten Knesset members of that party would probably support it. Moreover, depending on the terms of the agreement concerning Jerusalem, it is likely that 3 or 4 Knesset members of the Sephardic/Mizrahi Shas party would also support it. Lieberman's Israel Our Home party, which at the last minute chose not to join Netanyahu's government, could go either way on this issue, depending on the terms of the agreement. All of the other opposition parties would almost surely support any reasonable agreement. Based on this sort of analysis, a number of Israeli pundits have written that if an agreement came to a vote, it might well pass, despite the right-wing nature of the coalition government itself.

At the same time, given the make-up of this Netanyahu coalition and who he has appointed to key positions, there is no likelihood whatsoever that Israel, **left to itself,** is going to initiate any meaningful Two-State negotiations. The key words here are "left to itself." In fact, the Minister that he has appointed to coordinate all contacts with the Palestinians is on record as being opposed to a Two-State solution and in favor of rapid expansion of the building of new settlements.

With regard to the Palestinians, President Abbas, while supportive of opening new negotiations, is in a very weak position politically. The Palestinian Authority is more than five years overdue for an election, which seriously undermines his legitimacy. His failure to support, in any effective manner, rebuilding in Gaza or the provision of any support for the people in Gaza, have dramatically weakened public support for him in both the West Bank and Gaza. Without a commitment from the Israeli government to forgo settlement expansion during Two-State negotiations, Abbas would not be allowed to enter such a process, even if he wanted to – which is unlikely. So the issue turns on whether **outside pressure** on Israel could elicit a freeze on the expansion of settlements (while perhaps allowing modest building within existing settlements) and the beginning of serious Two-State negotiations.

Fatah and Hamas have formally agreed to the formation of a Unity Government composed of technocrats not associated with either party. However, that government has no role in Gaza and cannot really speak for the people there. Without an effective Palestinian Unity Government, Israel can with some legitimacy claim that there is no one with whom to negotiate who really represents the totality of the Palestinian people. At the same time, Israel and the U.S. have labeled Hamas to be a terrorist organization and refused to negotiate with it, or with any Unity Government in which it participates – unless Hamas meets three pre-conditions. (1) It agrees to foreswear violence of every sort. (2) It agrees to recognize the legitimacy of Israel. (3) It commits to support the implementation of all prior agreements (e.g. Oslo, etc.). Hamas has responded by saying:

> (1) It will agree to a "truce" of any reasonable length, up to say 5 to 10 years or more, so long as Israel is negotiating in good faith.

(2) It will not recognize the legitimacy of the State of Israel so long as Israel refuses to recognize the State of Palestine. But Hamas has stated that that such mutual recognition would be the goal of the negotiations.

(3) It will not commit to implementing the Oslo accords, since it claims that Israel had failed to implement a whole series of Oslo commitments. But it will agree to a *mutual* implementation of Oslo and other agreements.

These positions by Hamas apparently seem reasonable to most Palestinians (according to polls), but have been declared to be unacceptable by both Israel and the U.S. So for now, any negotiations involving Israel and the U.S. can only be with a weakened and somewhat isolated Fatah, even though they nominally can be conducted with a very weak Unity Government of technocrats. But it is clear that without the direct support of Hamas, any agreement would apply only to the West Bank. The hope of Abbas and the U.S. is that such an agreement implemented with regard only to the West Bank, if it were successful, would eventually be supported by the people in Gaza who would force Hamas to accept it. Hamas has said it will not attempt to block negotiations conducted by the Palestinian Authority on behalf of the Palestinians in both the West Bank and Gaza, **if** it is agreed that there will be a referendum of all Palestinians before such a negotiated agreement is implemented.

Hamas is in a very weak position due to the demise of the Islamist (Sunni) Morsi government and the rise to power of an anti-Islamist military government in Egypt that strongly opposes Hamas. Similarly, Hamas has alienated itself from Assad in Syria, which is supported by Shia Iran. It thus has lost its land-based lifelines to Iranian support, which had been essential. It also suffered great losses in the series of three wars with Israel in Gaza in six years. As a result, there are reports that Israel and Hamas are holding indirect talks, with Tony Blair (former Prime Minister of Britain and former Representative of the "Quartet" (the E.U., U.S., U.N. and Russia) serving as the intermediary. In fact, Blair is said to have resigned as the official Quartet Representative to give himself more freedom to mediate these talks. It is also reported that the basic deal being discussed is that Israel would agree to lift the blockade of Gaza in exchange for a Hamas agreement to a 10-year truce that would include all factions in Gaza. It is far too early to predict what the outcome of this effort will be.

(Some reviewers of earlier versions of this paper have objected to my failure to discuss in more detail the three wars that Israel has fought in Gaza within the last six years, including an examination of the causes for each and the extremely uneven nature of the conflicts and of the results. Such a discussion would also have to include such issues as the rocket attacks on Israel, the tunnels built from Gaza into Israel, what led up to these rocket attacks, the blockade of Gaza by Israel (and now Egypt) and the miserable conditions under which the people there are forced to live. But I have decided that this analysis needs to be the subject of a paper of its own.)

On the broader issue of movement toward a renewal of Two-State negotiations, on the Palestinian side, the minimal condition that Abbas must demand (or risk being immediately overthrown or killed) to enter into new negotiations would be an agreement by Israel to delay any further building on the West Bank, except within a few established settlements, and certainly no new settlements in East Jerusalem. For now there is no likelihood that the Netanyahu government would agree to that precondition without strong and persistent **outside** pressure.

Thus, there is a broadly shared understanding that neither a Two-State agreement, or even negotiations toward that, are likely to occur unless and until an American government, with international support from the European Union and Russia, takes a hard and strong position to pressure **both** sides, both politically and, if need be, economically. Israel is increasingly nervous about its growing international isolation. It requires a good deal of international trade and outside support. Right now, the U.S. pays for about one-third of the Israeli defense budget and in the event of any conflict, Israel requires immediate and extensive re-supply from the U.S. Similarly, the Palestinian Authority requires budgetary support from the U.S. and Europe and its internal security system depends crucially on U.S. support. Israelis are keenly aware of their growing isolation. They are deeply afraid of the Boycott, Divestiture and Sanctions (BDS) movement being mounted in the U.S. and Europe – even to the extent of passing tough laws to try to block it. While BDS has had little real impact, psychologically it is perceived to be very threatening.

Similarly, the Israeli press has written extensively about the American organization known as J-Street, which is against BDS, but which declares itself to be Pro-Israel and Pro-Peace, and is strongly in favor of pressuring both Israel and the Palestinians to move toward the creation of two states. The fact that J Street has growing influence in Congress (as shown in the recent lobbying efforts around the Iran nuclear agreement) and a strong presence on hundreds of American college campuses is something that Israel also worries about. (More than 1,100 student representatives from more than 100 colleges attended the last (2015) J-Street conference in Washington.) Jewish Voice for Peace is an organization that strongly supports BDS and also has a significant presence on U.S. campuses and now reports having over 200,000 members. These movements, and others (such as Partners for Progressive Israel) of Jewish students on campuses around the U.S., and their non-Jewish allies, deeply worry the Israeli leadership for what it portends for future support from the American Jewish community. The Jewish Reform Movement is the largest sector of the American Jewish community and it has been taking an ever stronger Two-State position and has publicly criticized Netanyahu. Israel perceives itself to be losing the ideological struggle within the American Jewish community upon which it is very dependent for both direct financial as well as political support. This is especially true among American Jews under age 40. Indeed surveys have shown that the majority of the American Jewish community is willing to cut the U.S. government a lot of slack if it were to choose to take strong steps to pressure both the Israelis and the Palestinians to move toward a Two-State agreement. The key issue may well turn out to be how hard the U.S. government is able and willing to pressure the two sides.

The Impact on the Peace Process of the Agreement with Iran regarding its Nuclear Program
The August 2015 agreement by the U.S. and six other major powers (Britain, France, Germany, the E.U., Russia, and China) with Iran over the latter's nuclear program has introduced a new element into the U.S. – Israeli relationship. (Recall our earlier discussion of Israel's opposition to this agreement and how it was based on appealing to fear.) Clearly the opposition of Netanyahu's government to this agreement and the Israeli efforts to intervene in American politics has strained Israel's relations, not only with the Obama Administration, but also with much of the American Jewish community. Recent (August 2015) polls indicated that more than 60% of the American Jewish community supported the agreement with Iran, while 70% of Jewish Israelis opposed it. The support for the agreement by American Jews under the age of 40 was even higher. Within the U.S., the American Israel Public Affairs Committee (AIPAC) strongly supported Netanyahu's opposition to the Iran Agreement, while J Street, Jewish Voice for Peace and other "pro-Israel/pro-peace" Jewish groups supported it. These groups and others spent millions of dollars in lobbying and advertising efforts. Given the tensions the Iran issue produced within the American Jewish community, between major elements of that community and the Obama Administration, and between Israel and the Obama Administration, one has to ask how likely it is that the current U.S. government will undertake a serious new initiative to encourage negotiations toward a Two-State solution during its last 18 months in office and while the next presidential election is underway.

I suspect this is not at all likely. On the other hand, given the increasing international isolation of Israel and the splintering of support among especially younger American Jews, it is remotely possible that Netanyahu might find it useful, even necessary, to reconsider his position in order to try to curry international favor by offering to enter into new Two-State negotiations. Indeed,there have been some recent hints of this from Netanyahu.
> See the article by Barak Ravid: *Netanyahu to Peace Activists: I'm ready to go to Ramallah to meet with Abbas, Haaretz*, Sept 1, 2015, and the article by Itamar Sharon: *Netanyahu says willing to meet Abbas for peace talks "right now," The Times of Israel*, Sept 1, 2015

This may be an effort to repair the damage he has done by his unsuccessful effort in the U.S. to block the Iran nuclear agreement. However, it is also quite likely that this is a cynical publicity effort that does not indicate any real desire to move toward a Two-State solution. It is essential to understand that Netanyahu is using code language in making the offer to talk when he says there will be no preconditions to starting talks. In clear language, this means that he is open to pursuing talks only if, at the same time, he is free to continue the expansion of settlement building in the West Bank and in East Jerusalem. To put it another way, he is willing to talk (perhaps forever), but he is unwilling to freeze settlement expansion in order to open and conduct a new round of Two-State talks. But he knows that this is unacceptable to the Palestinians. An oft cited parable is:

> It is like a large, strong, well-fed guy sitting down with a small, weak, under-fed guy to discuss the division of a pizza that is set between them. But then the large guy restrains the little guy from eating anything, while the large guy eats as much as he can, all the while talking about how to divide what remains of the pizza … as the big guy keeps eating.

As noted often in this paper, Jewish Israelis and Jewish Americans have a hard time viewing Israel as the large, strong guy in this scenario. Nevertheless, any contention that calling for negotiations while expanding settlements is a fair or reasonable basis for negotiations is patently absurd, and is viewed as such by virtually the entire international community. Such an Israeli offer cannot be viewed as sincere unless the terms of a freeze on settlement expansion is agreed to be the very first item to discuss, and under a tight timeline.

Conservative governments and peace negotiations

Interestingly, history has shown that it is often easier for a conservative, rightwing government, such as Netanyahu's, to take politically risky steps toward peace, than for liberal governments to do so. The reason is simple. If a rightwing government moves in the direction of peace, the leftwing and centrist parties generally will support the move. But if a left or even centrist government does so, then the rightwing opposition will oppose the move. So it was Nixon, not Kennedy or Johnson, that opened up U.S. relations with China. By the same token, it was Menachem Begin, the old terrorist leader and conservative, who negotiated and signed the peace treaty between Israel and Egypt in 1978. Yitzhak Rabin was a military commander in 1948, was head of the General Staff during the 1967 war, and served for years as the Israeli Defense Minister. It was his strong military credentials which in part provided the political room for him to sign the Oslo Agreements establishing the Palestinian Authority and to sign the peace treaty with Jordan. So it is not irrational to hope that the growing isolation from both the U.S. and Europe could compel Netanyahu to negotiate a Two-State agreement and that his conservative credentials and the composition of the Knesset could give him the political room to sign it and get it ratified. Similarly, a greatly weakened Fatah/Abbas and an ever more isolated Hamas might find it strategically useful, in part in order to curry favor and acceptance internationally, to enter into negotiations toward a Two-State solution. But, as noted just above, some severe restrictions on the building of new settlements would have to be the very first topic, and with a short timeline on the talks to set those restrictions.

The possibility that leadership in Two-State negotiations might switch to others than the U.S.

It is also important to note that the initiative for negotiations might, for the first time, **not** come from the U.S. There are strong indications that the French government has been considering applying pressure on Israeli and Palestinian leaders through the U.N. Security Council, and that there have been French efforts to secure, for the first time, U.S. backing for such a move. The tensions over the Iran nuclear agreement, including between the European governments which participated in crafting that agreement and the Netanyahu government, resulted in placing this effort on the "back burner" while the U.S. Congress debated the Iran nuclear agreement. But now that Congress has acted to allow the implementation of the Iran nuclear agreement, this French effort could be resuscitated quickly. In fact, in the face of information that the effort in the U.S. Congress to block implementation of the agreement has failed, it was announced that:

> *"Arab states, Mideast Quartet to meet as part of EU bid to restart Israeli-Palestinian talks,"* Robin Emmott, *Haaretz*, Sept. 5, 2015

The Mideast Quartet refers to U.S., E.U., U.N. and Russia. The Arab states involved in this effort are reported to be Egypt, Jordan and Saudi Arabia, and the head of the Arab League. Where such talks might lead is quite unclear as of this writing.

So Myth #15 could possibly prove to be too pessimistic and a way might be found to begin a new round of Two-State negotiations. However it seems clear that while this might have happened **if the U.S. applied enough pressure**, now, in the face of the turmoil caused by Israel's opposition to the Iran Agreement, it seems most

unlikely that this pressure from the U.S. will occur during the remaining months of the Obama Administration. Moreover, even if European governments were to try to foster new Two-State negotiations in the next year or so, the extreme anxiety within the Israeli Jewish population about Iran will continue to be heightened, perhaps purposely fanned, for some extended time. These anxieties may provide Netanyahu with the nationalistic support to resist any outside pressure to negotiate. In fact, some cynics have argued that for some years Netanyahu's focus on the danger posed by Iran, real or imaginary, was designed purposefully to provide a shield for him to resist Two-State negotiations while his government expanded the building of settlements. That is, Netanyahu understands all too well the inclination of Israeli Jews to think of themselves as weak and as potential victims, as we discussed earlier, and he intentionally plays upon that. The only question is whether the combination of some of the factors listed below might cause some rethinking in Israel. But this is a long shot at best.

- ✓ the increasing isolation of Israel internationally, especially from the E.U.
- ✓ the tensions Netanyahu has provoked within the America Jewish community
- ✓ the growing skepticism of American Jews under the age of 40 with regard to the policies and actions of the Israeli government
- ✓ the tensions created with the Obama Administration and the risks raised about the extent of U.S. support
- ✓ the weakening of the ability of traditional American Jewish organizations, such as the American Israel Public Affairs Committee (AIPAC), to offer effective, unconditional support for the Israeli government
- ✓ the growing influence in the American Jewish community of pro-peace, pro-Israel, pro-Two-State organizations such as J Street and Jewish Voice for Peace
- ✓ the growing Boycott, Divestiture and Sanctions (BDS) movement, including among major elements of the Christian community, internationally and in the U.S.

The Issue of the Charge of Anti-Semitism on the Prospects for a Two-State Agreement

One final consideration must be addressed. Successive Israeli governments, together with some major Jewish organizations in America and internationally, have far too successfully conflated criticism of actions by the Israeli government with anti-Semitism. Comments like those made by Netanyahu when he came to the U.S. to address the Iran nuclear agreement that he "speaks for all Jews" infuriated many American Jews -- leading to full-page advertisements in the New York Times and Washington Post sponsored by J Street saying that he did not speak for them. These very conscious and intentional efforts to deflect, even silence, criticism of Israeli government actions by claiming that such criticism is an attack on the right of Israel to exist, or that such criticism constitutes an attack upon all Jews, intentionally raises the specter of anti-Semitism in order to render the Israeli government immune from criticism. In fact, the critiques are often made by supporters of Israel and are intended to strengthen Israel. Moreover, they are virtually never addressed to the Jewish people as a whole. Thus, even by the standards established by the U.S. State Department (see below), such criticism does **not** constitute anti-Semitism.

Some major American organizations actively participate in this effort. Some even go so far as to claim that if one criticizes the Israeli government more than one criticizes other governments (such as Venezuela – and I have actually heard that comment), that is proof of anti-Semitism, that this is defamatory of the Jewish people as a whole. They simply refuse to accept (or cynically pretend to refuse to accept) that the Jewish people are not Israel, and that even the Israeli Jewish population is not the same as the Israeli government. But by claiming that critiques of Israeli government actions are critiques of Jews, by blurring the line between, on one hand, actions and beliefs of Jews generally with, on the other hand, actions and statements of the Israeli government, these organizations and the Israeli government are fostering the anti-Semitism they claim to oppose. By implying that actions by the Israeli government must be supported by all Jews, and that the Israeli government speaks for all Jews, these organizations and that government force a conflating of being Jewish and the Israeli government -- even when that government pursues what many around the world, including many American and Israeli Jews find objectionable, such as the treatment of Palestinians. In conflating being Jewish with these Israeli government policies, anti-Semitism is heightened, not ameliorated.

This tendency is visible when one studies the history that is the focus of this paper. In the view of such organizations and far too many of their supporters, to engage in the argument that the myths described above are to a very large extent false and misleading is, in their opinion, to undercut the legitimacy of the State of Israel, and therefore, by their definition, is proof of anti-Semitic views. Sustaining the mythological narratives is apparently viewed by these organizations/persons as essential to preventing the defamation of Jews generally, of Israel as a nation and of the Israeli government – a trinity they seem unable or unwilling to break apart. This pertains to the full panoply of myths about the history of Zionism, the manner in which the State of Israel was founded, the manner in which the Israeli War of Independence was fought, the nature of the modern Israeli government's behavior toward Palestinians both within Israel and in the occupied territories, and the conduct of negotiations with the Palestinians.

> Note –I would expect at this point to be challenged as to why I do not name the organizations to which I refer. This is quite intentional. I am not trying to pick a public fight with these groups. But if the shoe fits… I am quite certain that these groups and individuals recognize themselves quite easily in these comments. All I ask is that they at least seriously considered the points being raised and hopefully reconsider their rather casual and inappropriate use of the charge of anti-Semitism. And, I hope that those who are subjected falsely to the charge that they are being anti-Semitic keep these counter-arguments in mind.

In addressing the issue of anti-Semitism, the organizations and individuals who use this charge to deflect criticism of actions or policies of the Israeli government or to prevent the critical examination of the history of Israel, often cite the definition of anti-Semitism adopted by the U.S. State Department on June 8, 2010. This definition is quoted in full in **Appendix G**. In particular, they refer to the second part of the State Department's definition entitled: *What is Anti-Semitism Relative to Israel*. Here the State Department employs what has come to be known as the three Ds:

Demonize Israel, Double Standard for Israel, and Delegitimize Israel.

However, the State Department sets forth under each 'D' "Examples of ways in which anti-Semitism manifests itself with regard to the state of Israel, taking into account the overall context…" It is essential to read these carefully (see Appendix G) and note that these examples do **not** include criticisms of the behavior of the settlers/Israelis during their war of independence, **nor** criticisms of the manner in which the Israeli government treats Palestinians in Israel or in the Occupied Palestinian Territories.

When talking of the double standard, the State Department cites: "Applying double standards by requiring of it (Israel) a behavior not expected or demanded of any other democratic nation." Here I quite agree. Ethnic cleansing and the killing of unarmed civilians during a conflict are activities that are held to be unacceptable for all nations; therefore, providing evidence of this in the case of Israel is **not** evidence of anti-Semitism. Similarly, pointing out that Israel was not created by actions mandated by the United Nations General Assembly's recommended Partition Plan does not question the right of Israel to exist, but it does correct the record as to how Israel came to exist as a state. Hence this, too, is **not** anti-Semitic.

Moreover, under the terms of the international standard set forth in the Fourth Geneva Convention on the Rules of War, the

"resettlement by an occupying power of its own citizens on territory under its military control"

is forbidden and constitutes a violation of the Rules of War. Hence, to label the Israeli settlements on the West Bank or in East Jerusalem illegal is not to subject Israel to a double standard and is **not** anti-Semitic. Indeed, the U.N. General Assembly, the U.N. Security Council, the International Court of Criminal Justice, the International Committee of the Red Cross, and repeated meetings of the High Contracting Parties of the Geneva Convention have all ruled that these settlements are illegal and a breach of international law. Israel is the only nation which disputes these rulings and, using various rationales, simply claims that the Geneva Convention does not apply to what the U.N. officially labels the Occupied Palestinian Territory. But that claim by Israel does not provide any basis whatsoever to justify calling criticism of the settlement policy anti-Semitic.

> Note – The Geneva Convention is not to be confused with the Geneva Initiative or Geneva Agreement which was discussed earlier. The two sets of meetings just happened to have occured in the same city.

To cite another example: since criticism of the U.S., Argentina and Australia for how they dealt with their indigenous populations in the past, or deal with them today, is clearly quite common, it is totally improper to accuse someone of being anti-Semitic when that person criticizes the Israeli government for how it treated and treats the indigenous population of that land, the Palestinians. Moreover, one is not required to critique all nations in any given document. Quite the contrary, using the charge of anti-Semitism to deflect such critiques of Israeli history or of the Israeli government is evidence of the cynical misuse of the concept of anti-Semitism. Indeed, as explained above, such behavior actually may fan the flames of anti-Semitism.

It is quite important to note that the State Department ends its definition of anti-Semitism with regard to Israel with the statement:

> "However, criticism of Israel similar to that leveled against any other country
> **cannot** be regarded as anti-Semitic." (Emphasis added) (See Appendix G)

The focus of this paper is to examine these many myths, not simply as an exercise in historical analysis, but rather to explore the impact of the belief in these myths on the prospects for a Two-State Solution.   The same is true about why it is important to critically examine how the charge of anti-Semitism is used to deflect criticism of Israeli government policies. The particular relevance is that it is apparent to many around the world that strong pressure, diplomatic and probably economic, must be brought to bear upon the Israeli government **and** upon the Palestinian authorities if meaningful negotiations toward a Two-State solution are to occur, and if a resulting agreement is to be implemented. We shall see whether the cry of anti-Semitism will be effective in deflecting that pressure upon the Israeli government and preventing a Two-State solution from emerging. It seems to me that with regard to the Israeli government, it rests upon the shoulders of progressive Jews around the world, but especially in the U.S., to prevent this from happening. It is our responsibility to legitimize criticism of Israeli government policy and to make it clear that such criticism, by Jews and non-Jews alike, does **not** constitute anti-Semitism.

In a similar vein, Arabs, both Muslim and Christian, have the responsibility to legitimize critiques of the Palestinian authorities, to make clear the urgency of Palestinian support for movement toward Two-States, and to resist conflating such critiques with accusations of Islamophobia or anti-Arab sentiments.

I fear that if we do not make these distinctions clear, we will by our inaction render impossible the emergence of two states, Israel and Palestine, existing side-by-side in peace and security.

Appendixes

The Population Mix in Palestine before the Creation of Israel

Dates	Jewish		Christian		Muslim		Comments
	%	# in 1,000s	%	# in 1,000s	%	# in 1,000s	Comments
Before 300 CE	Majority are Jewish						
By 600 CE	25-30%		70-75%		Muslim "invasions" begin		
By 1200	Minority		Minority		Majority		
In 1300s population drops due to Black Death			But Ottoman Empire (Muslim) begins in 1299				
1530s	3.0%	5k	4.0%	6k	93.0%	145k	Note small numbers
1690	0.8%	2k	4.7%	11k	94.5%	219k	
1492	Jews expelled from Spain, following expulsions from England & France						
1800	2.5%	7k	8.0%	22k	89.5%	246k	
	Jews are a mix of Mizrahim and Sephardic, but virtually all consider themselves Arab Jews						
1881-90	Zionism begins in Eastern Europe - Ashkenazic Jews begin first wave of immigration to Palestine						
1890	8.0%	43k	11.0%	57k	81.0%	432k	
1914	13.6%	94k	10.2%	70k	76.2%	525k	Start of World War I
1931	17.1%	175k	8.7%	89k	74.2%	760k	Beginning of Nazism
1947	32.2%	630k	7.3%	143k	60.4%	1,191k	Beginning of War
UN Partition Plan proposes 55.5% of land to Jews, 44.3% to Palestinians, Jews occupied only 7% of land							

Before 1947-48 Civil War & 1948-49 Arab-Israeli War -- Together also called the Israeli War of Independence
Palestinians refer to this entire conflict as **Al Nakba - The Catastrophe**

        Palestinians included all of the Muslims and most of the Christians in Palestine: about 1.3 million

After the wars-1949

        156,000 Palestinians lived in Israel and eventually received citizenship,

            But many remaining in Israel had been displaced from their original homes and villages.

        711,000 (per U.N., commonly 750k) lived in 58 U.N. refugee camps around the Middle East

        More than 50,000 had fled to nations around the world, most having left by sea before 1948.

        About 383,000 remainded on the West Bank (Transjordan) or in Gaza (Egypt)

Appendix B
Population of Israel and Palestine in 2014
and Total Jewish and Palestinian populations

Palestinian Population

Living in Israel: 1.7 million (20.7% of Israeli pop. of 8.21 million)

Living in Palestine (West Bank & Gaza):   4.44 million (2.73m on West Bank, 1.71m in Gaza)

Living in U.N. camps in other countries: 1.4 million (U.N. gave refugee status to decendants)

Living outside Israel, Palestine, or camps: 5 million

Jewish Population

Living in Israel or in Settlements 6.2 million

   West Bank   356,000 (4.3% of total pop., 5.7% of Jewish pop.)

   East Jerusalem   290,000 (3.5% of total pop., 4.7% of Jewish pop.)

Living in U.S.: 5.7 million. In France, Canada & U.K.: 1.2 million.   Elsewhere: 0.8 million

Population of Mandate Palestine (that is, all of Israel, West Bank and Gaza):

      Jewish: 6.20 million, Palestinian 6.14 million -- virtually 50/50

       By 2020: Majority will be Palestinian

Two-State Solution per Geneva Initiative: 208,000 Jewish Setters on West Bank would be in Israel
and only 147,000 (1.8% of total pop.) would need to be moved or left in Palestine, their choice.
  If choose to remain in settlements in Palestine, would retain Israeli citizenship, but like any ex-pat
  would be subject to local, i.e.-Palestinian law.
Jewish "settlers" in East Jerusalem could remain in place with Israeli citizenship, but again under
  Palestinian administration, unless they are in what are designated as Jewish neighborhoods
  which are to be annexed into Israel
Palestinians living in East Jerusalem would become Palestinian citizens, and lose Israeli resident status.

Appendix C
The Geneva Initiative 2003 – Summary of Agreement

Accord principles:
- End of conflict. End of all claims.
- Mutual recognition of Israeli and Palestinian right to two separate states.
- A final, agreed upon border.
- A comprehensive solution to the refugee problem.
- Large settlement blocks and most of the settlers are annexed to Israel, as part of a 1:1 land swap.
- Recognition of the Jewish neighborhoods in Jerusalem as the Israeli capital and recognition of the Arab neighborhoods of Jerusalem as the Palestinian capital.
- A demilitarized Palestinian state.
- A comprehensive and complete Palestinian commitment to fighting terrorism and incitement.
- An international verification group to oversee implementation.

Description

The Geneva Initiative is a model permanent status agreement between the State of Israel and the State of Palestine. The accord presents a comprehensive and unequivocal solution to all issues vital to ensuring the end of the conflict. Adopting the agreement and implementing it would bring about a solution to the historical conflict, a new chapter in Israeli-Palestinian relations, and, most importantly, the realization of the national visions of both parties.

1. Mutual recognition:

As part of the accord, the Palestinians recognize the right of the Jewish people to their own state and recognize the State of Israel as their national home. Conversely, the Israelis recognize the Palestinian state as the national home of the Palestinian people.

2. Borders and settlements:
- The border marked on a detailed map is final and indisputable.
- According to the accord and maps, the extended borders of the State of Israel will include Jewish settlements currently beyond the Green Line, Jewish neighborhoods in East Jerusalem, and territories with significance for security surrounding Ben Gurion International Airport. These territories will be annexed to Israel on agreement and will become inseparable from it.
- In return to the annexation of land beyond the 1967 border, Israel will hand over alternative land to the Palestinian, based on a 1:1 ratio. The lands annexed to the Palestinian State will be of equal quality and quantity.

3. Jerusalem:
- The parties shall have their mutually recognized capitals in the areas of Jerusalem under their respective sovereignty.
- The Jewish neighborhoods of Jerusalem will be under Israeli sovereignty, and the Arab neighborhoods of Jerusalem will be under Palestinian sovereignty.
- The parties will commit to safeguarding the character, holiness, and freedom of worship in the city.
- The parties view the Old City as one whole enjoying a unique character. Movement within the Old City shall be free and unimpeded subject to the provisions of this article and rules and regulations pertaining to the various holy sites.
- There shall be no digging, excavation, or construction on al-Haram al-Sharif / the Temple Mount, unless approved by the two parties.
- A visible color-coding scheme shall be used in the Old City to denote the sovereign areas of the respective Parties.
- Palestinian Jerusalemites who currently are permanent residents of Israel shall lose this status upon the transfer of authority to Palestine of those areas in which they reside.

Appendix C - Geneva Initiative (continued)

4. International Supervision:

An Implementation and Verification Group (IVG) shall be established to facilitate, assist in, guarantee, monitor, and resolve disputes relating to the implementation of the agreement. As part of the IVG, a Multinational Force (MF) shall be established to provide security guarantees to the parties. To perform the functions specified in this agreement, the MF shall be deployed in the state of Palestine.

5. Refugees:

The agreement provides for the permanent and complete resolution of the Palestinian refugee problem, under which refugees will be entitled to compensation for their refugee status and for loss of property, and will have the right to return to the State of Palestine. The refugees could also elect to remain in their present host countries, or relocate to third countries, among them Israel, at the sovereign discretion of third countries.

6. Security:

Palestine and Israel shall each recognize and respect the other's right to live in peace within secure and recognized boundaries free from the threat or acts of war, terrorism and violence. Both sides shall prevent the formation of irregular forces or armed bands, and combat terrorism and incitement. Palestine shall be a non-militarized state, with a strong security force.

Party Name (Leader) Position on Relations with Palestinians, Two State Solution, Matrix of Control	Seats 120 Total (old #)	Cumulative (61 needed -- more if stable)
Likud (Netanyahu)	30 (18)	30
No real support for a political Two-State Solution, talks only of strengthening Palestinian economy, will expand settlements, maintain full Matrix of Control on West Bank.		
Kulanu (Kahlon)	10 (0)	40
Primarily concerned with domestic economic and social policy. Leader was a member of Likud and a Minister in former government. Wants to improve housing, health care, education. Not opposed to Two-States.		
The Jewish Home (Bennett)	8 (11)	48
This is the party of the Settlers, strongly opposes any move toward Two-States or the giving up of any land. Wants to expand settlements.		
Shas (Deri)	7 (11)	55
Sephardic – Mizrahim Ultra-Orthodox party – key issue is protection of rights/privileges of orthodox, no division of Jerusalem Under any circumstances, minimal pullback to create weak Two-States, and maintain full Matrix of Control. Religious marriage and divorce only		
United Torah Judaism (Litzman)	6 (7)	61
Ashkenazic Ultra-Orthodox party - key issue is protection of rights/ privileges of orthodox, religious control of marriage and divorce. No support for Two States, maintain full Matrix of Control		
The above have agreed to form the new coalition government under Netanyahu. This is perhaps the most rightwing in Israeli history. Parties below are in opposition (as of this writing).		
Yisrael Beiteinu (Israel Our Home) (Lieberman)	6 (15)	67
Expel Palestinian-Israeli citizens into weak Palestinian state via land swaps, hold & expand all major settlements, force remaining Palestinian-Israelis to take loyalty oath. Civil marriage & divorce. Was expected to join gov't, but refused at last minute. May join later.		
Zionist Union (Herzog & Livni) (Largest Opposition Party)	24 (21)	
New Party combines old Labor party and Livini's Hatnua party. Supports Settlement freeze except within major existing settlements and Two-State solution. Also focus on social and economic improvements and improving relations with U.S.		
Joint List (Odeh)	13 (11)	
Was three separate Palestinian parties, plus Communist Party (which is mixed Palestinian-Jewish) Parties represent interests of Palestinian-Israeli citizens. Strong support for Two-States and improvement of social economic conditions of Palestinian-Israelis.May not hold together		
Yesh Atid (Lapid)	11 (19)	
Leader was popular news anchor and writer. Primary focus on domestic social and economic issues, but strongly supports Two-State solution. Was Finance Minister in prior Likud/Netanyahu government.		
Meretz (Gal-On)	3 (5)	120
The "Peace Party" Two-State Solution, will deal with Palestinian Unity Gov't. Supports full settlement pullback & minimum Matrix of Control.		

Appendix E
Partition Plan Recommended by U.N. General Assembly, Nov. 1947
(Resolution # 181)

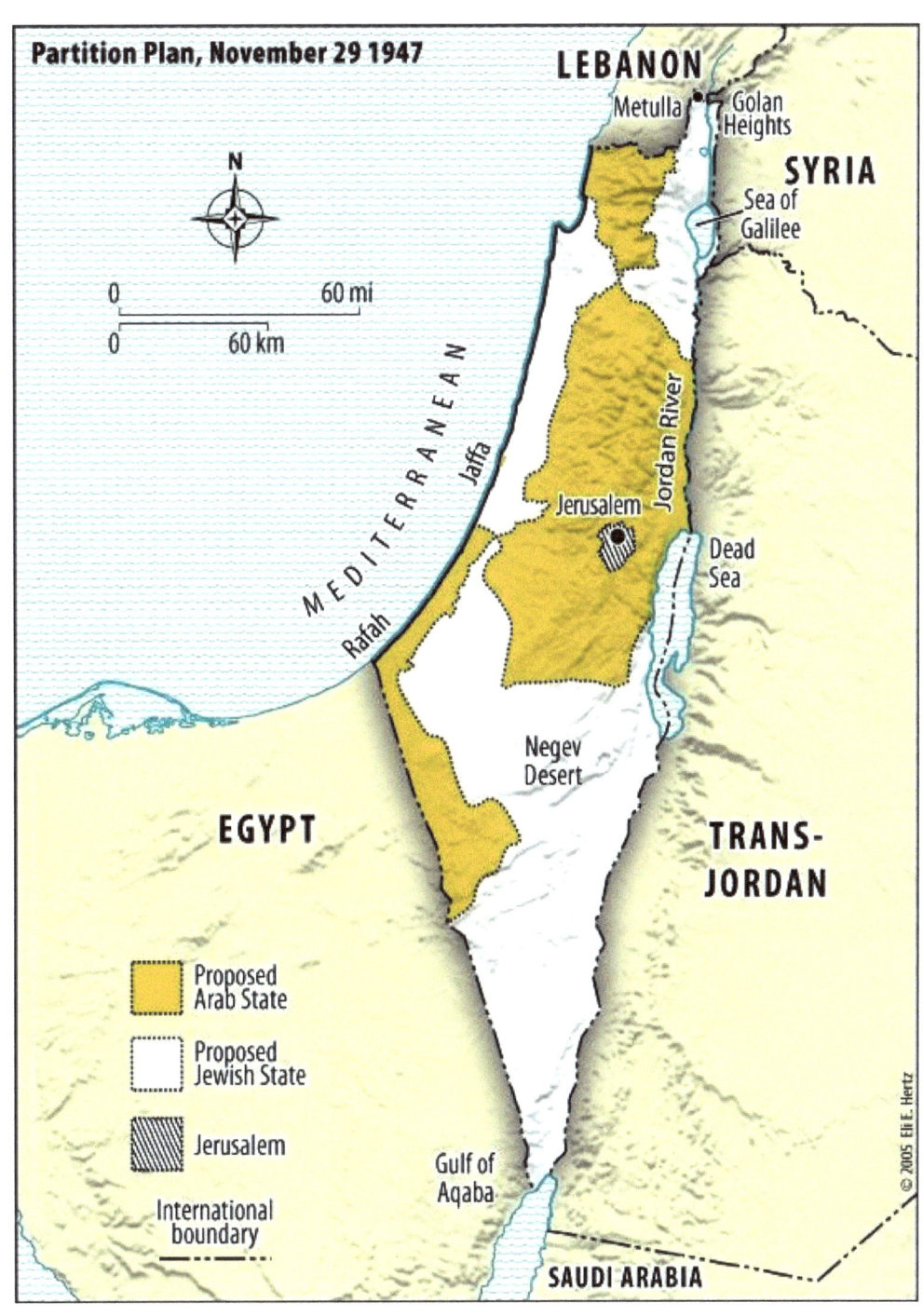

Source of map
https://www.google.com/search?q=partition+of+palestine+1948+maps&espv=2&biw=1352&bih=780&tbm=isch&tbo=u&source=UNiv&sa=X&ved=0CDsQsARqFQoTCN2qoOHBsccCFU9BiAod-bUAmA&dpr=1#imgrc=g0AkDQ_NcZrYGM%3A

Appendix F - Map of Results of 1947-49 Wars

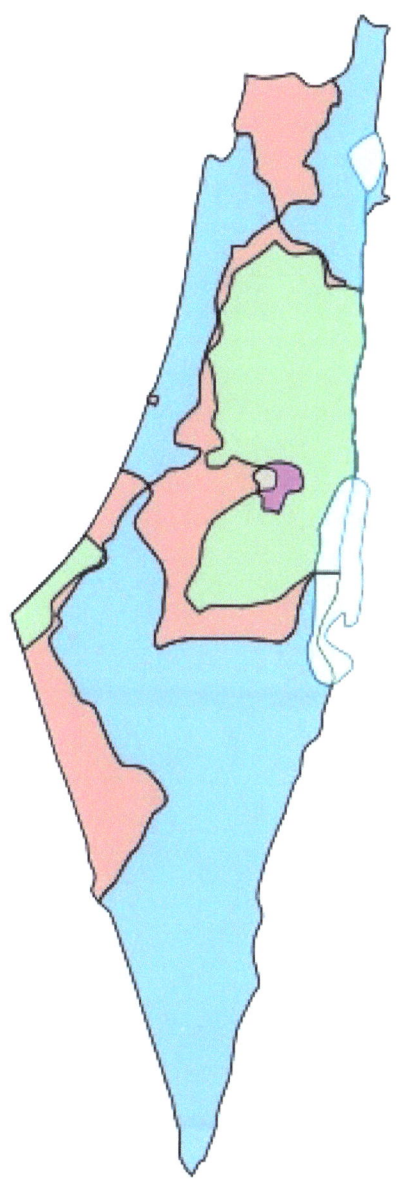

Green: Portion of Palestinian Partition Defined Territory that was retained by Arabs in 1949 after wars.
    But Gaza to Egypt, West Bank to Transjordan, <u>None</u> Under Palestinian control

Pink: Palestinian Partition Defined Territory captured by Israel.

Blue: Israeli Partition Defined Territory, all was kept by Israel

Purple: Partition Defined Jerusalem International Zone, captured and held by Transjordan

Beige: Partition Defined Jerusalem International Zone, captured and held by Israel

    Relative Size of Military Forces (including those invading Palestine from other five Arab nations);

There are many estimates, especially of the Arab forces, these seem to me the most accurate:

        July 1948: Israel: 63,000 - Arab: 48,000

        April 1949: Israel: 115,000 – Arab: 49,000

    Arab Maximum at any time: 51,000-63,000 Israeli Maximum: 117,500

Appendix G

U.S. State Department's Definition of Anti-Semitism and Statement of What is Anti-Semitism Relative to Israel

The State Department statement begins with the following quotation:

> "Anti-Semitism is a certain perception of Jews, which may be expressed as hatred toward Jews. Rhetorical and physical manifestations of anti-Semitism are directed toward Jewish or non-Jewish individuals and/or their property, toward Jewish community institutions and religious facilities." -- Working Definition of Anti-Semitism by the European Monitoring Center on Racism and Xenophobia

It then goes on to state:

Contemporary Examples of Anti-Semitism

Calling for, aiding, or justifying the killing or harming of Jews (often in the name of a radical ideology or an extremist view of religion).

Making mendacious, dehumanizing, demonizing, or stereotypical allegations about Jews as such or the power of Jews as a collective—especially but not exclusively, the myth about a world Jewish conspiracy or of Jews controlling the media, economy, government or other societal institutions.

Accusing Jews as a people of being responsible for real or imagined wrongdoing committed by a single Jewish person or group, the state of Israel, or even for acts committed by non-Jews.

Accusing the Jews as a people, or Israel as a state, of inventing or exaggerating the Holocaust.

Accusing Jewish citizens of being more loyal to Israel, or to the alleged priorities of Jews worldwide, than to the interest of their own nations.

What is Anti-Semitism Relative to Israel?

EXAMPLES of the ways in which anti-Semitism manifests itself with regard to the state of Israel, taking into account the overall context could include:

DEMONIZE ISRAEL:

Using the symbols and images associated with classic anti-Semitism to characterize Israel or Israelis

Drawing comparisons of contemporary Israeli policy to that of the Nazis

Blaming Israel for all inter-religious or political tensions

DOUBLE STANDARD FOR ISRAEL:

Applying double standards by requiring of it a behavior not expected or demanded of any other democratic nation

Multilateral organizations focusing on Israel only for peace or human rights investigations

DELEGITIMIZE ISRAEL:

Denying the Jewish people their right to self-determination, and denying Israel the right to exist

However, criticism of Israel similar to that leveled against any other country cannot be regarded as anti-Semitic. (emphasis added)

U.S. Department of State June 8, 2010 (http://www.state.gov/documents/organization/156684.pdf)

About the Author

Andrew Winnick has studied, lectured and written about the Israel-Palestine situation for over 40 years and has lectured widely in the U.S. and Europe. He has traveled often to Israel and the Occupied Palestinian Territory and met with Israeli and Palestinian activists in the peace movement there. For three years, he was an academic consultant to Bethlehem University. His work includes *U.S. Foreign Policy in the Middle East and the Israeli-Palestinian Conflict (2006); The Impact of the Israel-Hezbollah War on the Prospects for Peace in the Region (2007);The Prospect for a Two-State Solution between the Israelis and Palestinians Given the Current Situation in Gaza* (2008); *The Prospects for Success in the Israeli-Palestinian-U.S. Peace Talks* (2009); *A Brief History of Israeli and Palestinian Nationalism and the Identification of Crucial Current Issues in Palestinian-Israeli Relations* (2009); *The Histories of Palestinian and Jewish Nationalism and the Current Prospects for Peace (2012).* He is also the author of *A Secular Haggadah,* which has been re-edited annually for more than 30 years and used at Passover by Jewish families in the U.S. and Europe. A major theme of this Haggadah is the relevance of Jewish history to a critical understanding of the history of Israeli-Palestinian relations. He is a member of J-Street, Americans for Peace Now, Jewish Voice for Peace and Friends of Sabeel North America. He is a founding member of The Working Group for Middle East Peace, an interfaith organization that has sponsored an interfaith Seder for the past eight years in which Jewish, Christian and Muslim congregations come together at a mosque to celebrate Passover. They also sponsor film showings and lectures on Israel-Palestine. He authored the book *The Changing Distributions of Income and Wealth in the U.S.* He considers himself to be a Political Economist, working at the interface of economics, political science, sociology and history, and has taught in all these areas. He is currently a Professor of Economics and Statistics at California State University-Los Angeles and has held regular and visiting professorships and academic administrative positions at a number of other universities. He is the founding president of The American Institute for Progressive Democracy (see taipd.org), a think-tank in Claremont, CA.